Standards-Based Leadership

A Case Study Book for the Superintendency

Sandra Lowery
and Sandra Harris

A SCARECROWEDUCATION BOOK

The Scarecrow Press, Inc.
Lanham, Maryland, and Oxford
2003

A SCARECROWEDUCATION BOOK

Published in the United States of America
by Scarecrow Press, Inc.
A Member of the Rowman & Littlefield Publishing Group
4501 Forbes Boulevard, Suite 200, Lanham, Maryland 20706
www.scarecroweducation.com

PO Box 317
Oxford
OX2 9RU, UK

British Library Cataloguing in Publication Information Available

Library of Congress Cataloging-in-Publication Data

Lowery, Sandra Lynn Tillman, 1944–
  Standards-based leadership : a case study book for the superintendency /
Sandra Lowery, Sandra Harris.
     p. cm.
"A ScarecrowEducation book."
Includes bibliographical references and index.
  ISBN 0-8108-4608-X (pbk. : alk. paper)
  1. School superintendents—United States. 2. Educational leadership—
United States 3. Education—Standards—United States. I. Harris, Sandra,
1946– II. Title.
LB2831.72 .L69 2003
371.2'011—dc21

                                  2002012352

∞™ The paper used in this publication meets the minimum requirements of
American National Standard for Information Sciences—Permanence of
Paper for Printed Library Materials, ANSI/NISO Z39.48-1992.
Manufactured in the United States of America.

Contents

Foreword

Sandra Lowery and Sandra Harris have created an exciting new book on the changing, challenging role of the superintendency. These real-world and scary case studies are centered on actual events faced by school superintendents in small, medium, and large school districts. Drawing on leading research and best practice about the superintendency, Drs. Lowery and Harris lead the reader through the power of reflective action in decision making and case study methods that "provide leaders with a framework in which to examine their own values and test these values within the organizational setting." In addition, the authors present strategies for discussing the case study, evaluation of the strategies, and specific steps in making the best decisions for positive solutions.

This book is far more than case studies because each case is linked to state and national standards for the preparation and licensure of system administrators. The Texas standards, which are a slight adaptation of the *Professional Standards of the Superintendency* (AASA), are the guiding principles, followed by sets created by the National Council for Accreditation of Teacher Education (NCATE), and the Interstate School Leaders Licensure Consortium (ISLLC). Each chapter and case study is linked to these standards to guide professors in aligning the standards for licensure examinations, for NCATE program approval, and for raising the bar in the quality of preparation and professional development of system school administrators.

In addition, this book provides an excellent model for problem-based learning called for in *Superintendents for Texas School Districts: Solving the Crisis in Executive Leadership,* sponsored by the Sid Richardson Foundation Forum and distributed throughout all states and Canada (Hoyle, 2002). This report recommends, "Projects in the preparation programs should be closely aligned with the data from actual school districts, which address the real issues that exist. More problem-based and data-driven curriculum grounded in sound theory are vital to successful performance in the dynamic world of the superintendency." The case studies in this new book will enliven classroom discussion and challenge the professional ethics of aspiring and practicing system administrators.

Finally, Sandra Lowery and Sandra Harris have battle scars from public school classroom teaching, campus administration, and the superintendent "hot seat." When they talk, students and colleagues listen. Both authors are active in the Texas Association of School Administrators and the American Association of School Administrators (AASA), and are frequent presenters at the National Conference of Professors of Educational Administration and other professional conferences. They are making a difference in the preparation and nurturing of school superintendents. Their book is a must to assist students in grappling with the real issues of the superintendency and in passing state licensure examinations.

John R. Hoyle, Ph.D.
Texas A & M University

REFERENCE

Hoyle, J. (2002). *Superintendents for Texas School Districts: Solving the crisis in executive leadership.* Fort Worth, TX: Sid W. Richardson Foundation.

Introduction

The role of the school superintendent is filled with external pressures often played out in the arena of public criticism. This role has undergone significant change in recent years, and today there is more emphasis on curriculum and instruction, planning for the future, involving others in decision making, improving student achievement (Short and Scribner, 2000), managing fiscal resources (Thompson, Wood, and Honeyman, 1994), and building cultural leadership (Schwahn and Spady, 1998). In fact, Houston (2001) writes that the superintendent must provide the "final answer" (p. 429) while being responsible for all aspects of the organization. Certainly, superintendents are not strangers to controversy (Dennis, 1997), especially as the superintendency has become more and more a political job that must respond to diverse community needs (Keedy and Bjork, 2001).

Today superintendents must face conflict over values and interests, increased political activism, challenges to purposes and goals of education, and many other issues (Keedy and Bjork, 2001). At the same time, superintendents have many tremendous opportunities to change children's lives, alter organizations, and influence entire communities (Houston, 2001). In fact, Education Secretary Rod Paige asserts that "there is no more important job than that of leading effective public schools" (Paige, 2001, p. 26). Yet, as the demands for accountability are heightened and the expectations are more and more unrealistic, leaders are less interested in becoming superintendents or staying in this role once they have been in it for several years (Goodman and Zimmerman, 2000; Houston, 2001).

WHAT IS SO DIFFICULT ABOUT THE JOB
OF THE SUPERINTENDENT?

Clearly, the opportunities to do this important job of the superintendency are fraught with difficulties that include rapidly changing community demographics (Houston, 2001), increased community political activism (Keedy and Bjork, 2001), and increased accountability measures (Mathews, 2001). Callahan's vulnerability theory (1962) focused primarily on school board difficulty, and Lutz (1990) extended this theory to include dissatisfaction reasons within the community. Greyser (1999) suggested the role of the superintendent often leads to isolation as administrators move up the leadership ladder. While leaders often put unrealistic demands on themselves to have all the right answers, still, inspiring leadership for excellence is at the heart of the superintendency (Hoyle, English, and Steffy, 1998).

The term "stress" is often associated with the superintendency. In fact, a survey of retired school superintendents in New York cited stress as the most common reason for their decision to retire (Goldstein, 1992). Districts that have difficult political situations, little money, poor staff morale, and poor student achievement are especially stressful (Goldstein, 1992). Brubaker and Coble (1995) suggest that subtle contradictions, for example, the expectation that a superintendent will cultivate a reputation as a leader who is authoritative, yet avoid appearing authoritarian, are inherently stressors in the job. On the other hand, Milstein (1992) suggests that while educational administrators believe their work is full of stress, the research suggests that most cope with it quite well. Simply put, even though within the last twenty-five years many efforts have been made to improve schools, superintendents face situations for which there are no easy answers (Goodman and Zimmerman, 2000).

Recruitment and Retention Problems

According to a recent American Association of School Administrators (AASA, 2000) study, the overall median age of public school superintendents is 52.5 years old. Thus, as the current slate of practicing school superintendents ages, there are indications that there is a growing shortage of qualified individuals to fill the positions they leave vacant. In fact, one recent survey reported that 80 percent of the superintendents who responded were eligible for retirement (Cooper, 2000). The Illinois State Board of Education recently issued a report indicating that in the next three years 47 percent of current school administrators will become eligible for retirement (Rohn, 2001).

Another Illinois report predicted that at least 40 percent of current superintendents will be retiring in the next five years (Pierson and Hall, 2001). Patterson (2000) interviewed fourteen superintendents, and two years later, 75 percent of these individuals had left the superintendency altogether. Additionally, Rohn (2001) reported that as disconcerting as the retirement numbers are, Illinois school board members have identified a related concern—the size and quality of the candidate pool is shrinking.

The shortage in the pool of superintendent candidates is even more pronounced when one considers the number of minority individuals who enter the superintendency. Nationwide, 88 to 90 percent of all school superintendents in the United States are men (Skrla, 2001; Hodgkinson & Montenegro, 1999). While the number of women superintendents is increasing from only 1 percent in 1967 (Stoker, 1967) to 13.6 percent in 2000 (AASA, 2000), this is still low considering that 75 percent of teaching positions are held by women (Skrla, 2001).

While there are many reasons for the low numbers of women currently holding superintendency positions, Allen (1996) reported that family concerns often serve as a barrier, and Ramsey (1997) asserted that family support is necessary for women to succeed as superintendents. Politics are also seen as a barrier, because women seem to be less tolerant of the politics found in the role of the superintendent.

At the same time, men and women of color are also seriously underrepresented in the superintendency with only 5 percent of these positions held by minority individuals (Glass, Bjork, and Brunner, 2000; AASA, 2000). Jones and Montenegro (1983) assert that only since the early 1950s have school districts been represented by superintendents who were African American, Hispanic, or Asian American. Yet only 3 percent of school administrators (this includes principals, as well as superintendents) are Hispanic, and only 8 percent are African American (*Digest of Educational Statistics*, 1990). Typically, these individuals serve in districts where persons of the same race are represented in significant numbers

(AASA, 1983). Also, Zemlicka (2001) found that minority superintendents held more educational positions prior to the superintendency, thus taking longer to achieve the position of superintendent.

Contributing to the superintendent shortage is that the average tenure of a superintendent in the United States is a mere five to six years (Glass, 1992; Hodgkinson and Montenegro, 1999). Chance and Capps (1990) studied the high turnover rates for superintendents within rural areas of Oklahoma and found that forty-one rural school districts had three or more superintendents in the last five years. Forty-three percent of the sixty-three superintendents who left rural districts were either terminated or forced to resign. The current annual turnover rate in Texas is between 20 and 25 percent with 272 superintendent vacancies out of the state's 1,050 school districts during the 1998–1999 school year (Moses, 2000). Even more disconcerting, Deary (1989) reports that in Connecticut nearly one-third of the turnover was involuntary, while 15 percent is more in line with the national average. An interesting finding regarding tenure is reported by Largent (2001) who found that Texas superintendents hired by a local school board had tenures nearly two years longer (5.85 years) than those hired through other processes, such as search consultants (3.97 years).

WHY WOULD ANYONE WANT TO BE A SUPERINTENDENT?

Houston (2001) reported that most superintendents find the job "exhilarating and challenging" (p. 429). In fact, many who leave the job actually come back to it in order to work in a job that offers opportunity to "change the trajectory of children's lives, alter the behavior of organizations, and expand the possibilities of whole communities" (p. 429). Patterson (2000) has noted that the superintendency is not just a job, but a lifestyle filled with important professional and personal accomplishments. It is an opportunity to do "difficult but valuable work" (p. 23) and to overcome challenges. Through professional reflection, many longtime superintendents have been able to ask hard questions and face the answers, thus contributing to their decision to stay on the job for the long haul (Kearns and Harvey, 2001).

Considering the difficult nature of the job, the difficulty of recruiting and retaining good superintendents, and the critical importance of this role, it is important that university training programs train superintendents in the reality of the job. It is equally important that practicing superintendents have resources available to them for continued learning while in the field. Utilizing the case study format for initial training and for "on-the-job" continued training can help accomplish this need.

EXPLANATION OF CASE STUDY FORMAT: THE ROLE OF REFLECTION

Traditionally, educator preparation programs have been structured on the premise that learning to be an educator is a process of acquiring teacher/administrator knowledge, "deposit-making" as opposed to posing the problems of human beings in their relation with the world (Freire, 1992, p. 60). Even in a comprehensive review of research on learning how to teach, Wideen, Mayer-Smith, and Moon (1998) found that new teachers are most concerned about survival and rarely engage in "reflective action" (p. 153). This scenario is frequently the case whether the program is a teacher preparation program or an administrator preparation program: students are not able to connect university classroom learning with the real experiences in [education] (Harris, 2000).

However, assumptions inherent in the andragogical model of learning point out that learners enter educational programs with a great diversity of experience (Knowles, 1990) and that learning from experiences is a unique meaning-making event (Kasworm and Marienau, 1997). In fact, Harris (2000) studied the responses of twenty-eight administrator preparation students regarding their participation in reflective writing activities that were connected to real-life experiences. Students collectively agreed that "real life meaning [came] from sharing educational experiences" (p. 24).

As individuals construct meanings from their own experiences (Dewey, 1938; Schon, 1987), the idea of reflection-in-action becomes knowing-in-action (Schon, 1987). Thus, reflecting on experiences of the school day is valuable as it leads to trying out new actions, testing understandings, affirming or changing decisions, legitimizing the memory, and leading to experience as a resource for educating professionals (Clandinin and Connelly, 2000). In fact, Clandinin and Connelly (1994) suggest that "to study education . . . is to study experience. . . . Experience is the stories people live" (p. 415).

Using Standards in the Reflection Process

In addition to making decisions by reflecting on one's experiences, an equally important component of reflection that leads to quality decision making is that of using standards as a framework. Standards for advanced programs in educational leadership were developed by the National Policy Board for Educational Administration (NPBEA) on behalf of the National Council for the Accreditation of Teacher Education (NCATE), which accredits schools and colleges of education. At the same time, the Interstate School Leaders Licensure Consortium (ISLLC) standards were adopted by many states for the licensure of school administrators.

The most recent revision of NCATE guidelines have been integrated within the ISLLC standards framework ("Standards for Advanced Programs. . .," 2002). In some cases, states have chosen to create their own standards guidelines for educators. For example, the Texas State Board of Educator Certification (SBEC) has adopted standards for educators, including guidelines for teachers, principals, and superintendents. These standards are divided into three domains: leadership of the educational community, instructional leadership, and administrative leadership.

NCATE, ISLLC, and Texas Standards identify larger goals as proficiencies, or competencies, that are broken down into smaller behavioral components that are outcomes based. Thus, when educators reflect in order to make good decisions, it is important that their reflections are guided by standards, rather than just their own experiences. Table I.1 shows a rubric detailing each chapter in the book and the various standards and topics that apply to each case study.

CASE STUDY METHODS

A case describes an administrative situation that involves a decision or a problem (Erskine, Leenders, and Mauffette-Leenders, 1981). Shulman (1996) describes case methods where students focus on real problems, developing a repertoire to guide their thinking and reflections on their own actions. Their own experiences become "lenses for thinking about their work" (p. 199), since analyzing the how and why of experiences is critical to effective, substantive, and enduring learning (Shulman, 1996). The very act of reflecting on experience implies a preparation for the future (Clandinin and Connelly, 1991), because it guides

Table I.1 Standards and Topics as They Apply to Case Studies

Chapter/Title	Standards: TEXAS	ISLLC	NCATE	Key Topics
1-Alyssa & Jenna	001 Act with integrity, fairness, ethical manner for success of all	5	5	leadership, ethics
2-Emperors New Clothes?	002 Shape district culture by facilitating, developing, articulating, implementing, and stewardship of vision of learning shared and supported by all	1	1	shared vision, site-based decisions, community relations
3-Blytheville	003 Communicate and collaborate with family and community, respond to diverse community interests/needs and mobilize resources for success of all	4	4	communication, diversity, social capital
4-Politics	004 Respond to and influence political, social, economic, legal, and cultural; work with board to achieve district's educational vision	6	6	school board, politics, change, conflict mgmt.
5-Higher Test Scores?	005 Plan and implement strategic plans for teaching and learning; align curriculum, resources, and assessment; promote varied assessments to measure student performance	2	2	planning, analyze data, instructional program, high-stakes testing
6-Se Habla Español Aqui	006 Advocate, nurture, sustain instructional program and culture for student learning and staff professional growth	2	2	culture, instructional leadership, bilingual
7-Oops! Technology Problems	007 Implement staff evaluation, and develop system to improve staff performance; select supervision and staff development	2	2	adult learning, technology, staff development
8-Make-Believe Budget	008 Apply principles of effective leadership and management to budgeting, personnel, resource utilization, financial management and technology	3	3	budget management, school financing
9-Contaminated Ground	009 Apply principles of leadership and management to physical plant and support systems for safe, effective learning environment	3	3	crisis management, safe schools
10-Accusations—True or False?	010 Apply organizational decision-making and problem-solving skills to facilitate positive change in varied contexts	1	1	decision-making, org. management, sexual harassment

metacognitive processes and guides future action (Brubacher, Case, and Reagan, 1994). Because so many problems that educators face are open-ended, a key value of reflection is that it offers a "process of solving problems, making decisions, and settling direction" (p. 91). While the case study method has been used in law, business administration, medicine, and counseling, it has only recently begun to have a place in educational administration. Although, since the mid-1950s simulations and in-basket activities (a form of case studies) have been used, the lecture method remains the primary instructional delivery model in school administration (McCarthy, 1999).

The case study method provides opportunities for administrators in preparation for the role of superintendent, as well as practicing superintendents, to role-play the conflicts in administrative decision making. Case studies provide leaders with a framework in which to examine their own values and to test these values within the organizational setting and the larger community setting. Cases allow students, through the simulation of an activity, to "explore approximations of reality" in individual reflection and group dialogue. Even more important, the case enables the learner to "examine a base of data that stands still for examination" (Storey, 2001, p. 7).

The case study method serves several purposes when used in a classroom setting. One purpose is that of teaching new information inductively, by having students read a case that models the concept and then note associations between certain factors. Another is as a critical-thinking, problem-solving vehicle for applying acquired knowledge to specific situations (Kowalski, 2001). Still another purpose is to develop the skill of synthesizing information through being asked to combine a variety of factors—time, ideas, data, community gatekeepers, and many others in the process of decision making. Clearly, the case study method provides an opportunity for students and practicing administrators to build a repertoire of skills in dealing with open-ended problems that characterize administration today.

STRATEGIES FOR DISCUSSING THE CASE STUDY

Kowalski (1999) reports that leaders, when confronted with problems demanding action, may choose one of several behaviors: ignoring the situation, acting instinctively, getting someone else to decide, duplicating something that someone else has done under similar circumstances, or using the professional knowledge base to guide decisions. It is important when using case studies as a learning strategy that participants have a clear understanding that there may not be *one* best answer to the case. Instead, with active participation of everyone in the class, discussion should generate several ways to consider the problem, and, likely, several different ways to solve it. This is especially true in considering the role of leadership due to the complex nature of the superintendency.

The rational-analytical model is a paradigm that lends itself to decision-making strategies with case studies with four steps (Romm and Mahler, 1986). These steps are define the problem, diagnose the problem, search for alternative solutions, and evaluate alternative solutions. Using these four strategies to guide the case study procedure, we recommend that the following steps be used for each case study:

Create a Climate of Trust within the Classroom

In order to fully and openly analyze each case study, it is important that the facilitator create a climate of trust within the classroom. Students should be encouraged to be creative, have the freedom to risk an idea, and be able to fail without fear of repercussion in the classroom setting. For problem solving to be most effective, it must occur within this environment of trust.

Read the Case Carefully

Good reading strategies should be followed. First, read to get a clear sense of the issue. Then, re-read, underlining or highlighting key ideas, and take notes in the margins or on a separate sheet of paper.

Identify the Primary Problem

While the case may describe many problems, it is important to analyze the case to identify the central problem at hand. By considering the central problem through the guidelines of the standards within which each of these cases is framed, it will be easier to isolate the primary issue of concern and determine appropriate actions.

Identify Related Problems

This is an important point. Too often in decision making, we attempt to solve the immediate problem, without considering the primary issue. For example, if teachers are arguing about a curriculum issue and it is causing disruption on the entire campus, this could be treated as a communication problem. However, upon further analysis, one would see that it is more than a communication problem, it is primarily a problem in faculty not having a shared vision of the school's purpose.

Discuss the Problem by Relating It Back to the Standard

What is the standard at issue here? If this is primarily a "shared vision" problem, be familiar with what the standards have to say regarding how to implement that standard on one's campus. The standards are based on best practices and grounded in the literature. Become familiar with the behavioral components of the standards because these are examples of the guiding actions that one would take.

Discuss the Problem by Relating It Back to the Literature

It is important in class discussion and analysis that students are guided back to the literature based on research for support. This gives the dialogue an impetus of legitimacy and leads to "best practice" strategies, rather than focusing entirely on one's "opinion" based on personal experiences alone.

Develop Strategies

When developing strategies based on case study information, it is helpful to identify circumstances where those strategies will be most likely to be successful. For example, the same problem may occur in a very small district and in a very large district. However, some strategies for responding to varying circumstances will, most likely, be very different. In other words, do not settle when one possible strategy has been identified. Develop alternative strategies also.

Evaluate Strategies

Carefully consider strategies that have been identified. What are the strengths of each suggestion, and what are the weaknesses? How could one best overcome inherent challenges within a situation?

Make a Decision

The role of leadership is decisive. One must be able to make a decision, support the decision, and outline specific strategies for implementation that will best help reach a positive solution.

HOW TO USE THIS BOOK

The ten case studies included in this book use the following structure: (1) identification of major competencies and standards; (2) abstract; (3) objectives; (4) brief literature review; (5) case; (6) discussion/ questions; (7) references; and (8) additional resources. Students are encouraged to discuss each case within the framework of the major competencies and standards, at first. As the discussion becomes more in-depth, certainly, other competencies and standards will contribute substantially to the case, as it is rarely possible to isolate strategies to just one area of standard.

REFERENCES

Allen, E. (1996). Why women exit the superintendency in Texas. (Doctoral dissertation, Baylor University, 1996). *Dissertation Abstracts International, 57*, No. 10A, 4195.

American Association of School Administrators. (1983). *Perspectives on racial minority and women school administrators.* Arlington, VA: American Association of School Administrators.

American Association of School Administrators. (2000). *The study of the American school superintendency 2000.* Arlington, VA: American Association of School Administrators.

Brubacher, J. W., Case, C. W., & Reagan, T. G. (1994). *Becoming a reflective educator: How to build a culture of inquiry in the schools.* Thousand Oaks, CA: Corwin Press.

Brubaker, D., and Coble, L. (1995). The derailed superintendent. *The Executive Educator, 17*(10), 34–36.

Callahan, R. (1962). *Education and the cult of efficiency: A study of the social forces that have shaped the administration of the public schools.* Chicago: University of Chicago Press.

Chance, E., and Capps, J. (1990). *Administrator stability in small/rural schools: The school board perspective.* Paper presented at the 82nd annual meeting of the National Rural Education Association, Colorado, Springs, CO, October 5–8, 1990.

Clandinin, D. J., and Connelly, F. M. (1991). Narrative and story in practice and research. In D. Schon (Ed.), *The reflective turn: Case studies in and on educational practice* (pp.258–281). New York: Teachers College Press.

Clandinin, D. J., and Connelly, F. M. (1994). Personal experience methods. In N. K. Denzin and Y. S. Lincoln (Eds.), *Handbook of qualitative research* (pp. 413–427). Thousand Oaks, CA: Sage Publications.

Clandinin, D. J., and Connelly, F. M. (2000). *Narrative inquiry: Experiences and story in qualitative research.* San Francisco: Jossey-Bass Publishers.

Cooper, B. (2000). Career crisis in the superintendency. In J. Natt (Ed.), *Superintendents see shortage of applicants for top spots as serious crisis.* Arlington, VA: American Association of School Administrators. Available online: www.aasa.org/archives/publications/in/01_00/01-27-00supecrisis.htm [accessed November 25, 2002].

Deary, J. (1989). Decision making and superintendent turnover: An empirical test of the Vroom and Yetton model with selected superintendents and board chairpersons in Connecticut. (Doctoral dissertation, University of Bridgeport, 1989). *Dissertation Abstracts International, 50,* 08A.

Dennis, B. (1997). When zealots wage war. *The School Administrator, 54*(2), 26–33.

Dewey, J. (1938). *Logic: The theory of inquiry.* New York: Henry Holt.

Digest of Educational Statistics. (1990). Washington, DC: National Center for Education Statistics, U.S. Department of Education.

Erskine, J., Leenders, M., and Mauffette-Leenders, L. (1981). *Teaching with cases.* London, Ontario: School of Business Administration, University of Western Ontario.

Freire, P. (1992). *Pedagogy of the oppressed* (20th ed.). New York: Continuum.

Glass, T. (1992). *The 1992 study of the American school superintendency.* Arlington, VA: American Association of School Administrators.

Glass, T., Bjork, L., and Brunner, C. (2000). *The study of the American superintendency 2000: A look at the superintendent of education in the new millennium.* Arlington, VA: American Association of School Administrators.

Goldstein, A. (1992). Stress in the superintendency. *The School Administrator, 49*(9), 8–13.

Goodman, R., and Zimmerman, W. (2000). *Thinking differently: Recommendations for 21st century school board/superintendent leadership, governance, and teamwork for high student achievement.* Arlington, VA: Educational Research Service

Greyser, L. (1999). Professional development helps counter lone ranger syndrome. *Leadership News, 1*(11).

Harris, S. (2000). The use of experience in reflective scenarios in administrator preparation. *Journal of the Intermountain Center for Educational Effectiveness, 1*(2), 20–27.

Hodgkinson, H., and Montenegro, X. (1999). *The U.S. school superintendent: The invisible CEO.* Washington, DC: Institute for Educational Leadership.

Houston, P. (2001). Superintendents for the 21st century: It's not just a job, it's a calling. *Phi Delta Kappan, 82*(6), 428–433.

Hoyle, J. R., English, F. W., and Steffy, B. E. (1998). *Skills for successful 21st century school leaders.* Arlington, VA: American Association of School Administrators.

Jones, E. and Montenegro, X. (1983). *Perspectives on racial minority and women school administrators.* Arlington, VA: American Association of School Administrators.

Kasworm, C. E., and Marienau, C.A. (1997). Principles for assessment of adult learning. *New Directions for Adult and Continuing Education, 75,* 5–16.

Kearns, D., and Harvey, J. (2001). *A legacy of learning.* Washington, DC: Brookings Institute Press.

Keedy, J., and Bjork, L. (2001). The superintendent, local boards, and the political arena. *The AASA Professor, 24*(4), 2–5.

Knowles, M. S. (1990). *The adult learner: A neglected species* (4th ed.). Houston: Gulf.

Kowalski, T. (1999). *The school superintendent: Theory, practice and cases.* Upper Saddle River, NJ: Prentice Hall.

Kowalski, T. (2001). *Case studies on educational administration* (3rd ed.). New York: Longman.

Largent, J. (2001). *Superintendent tenure: Characteristics of Texas superintendents, the school community, and their effect on tenure.* Unpublished dissertation. Sam Houston State University.

Lutz, F. 1990. Reforming education American style. In W. E. Eaton (Ed.), *History, politics and methodology in American education* (pp. 116–134). New York: Teachers College Press.

Mathews, J. (2001). Nontraditional thinking in the central office. *The School Administrator, 58*(6), 12–17.

McCarthy, M. (1999). The evolution of educational leadership preparation programs. In L. Murphy and K. Louis (Eds.), *Handbook of research on educational administration* (2nd ed.). San Francisco: Jossey-Bass.

Milstein, M. (1992). The overstated case of administrator stress. *The School Administrator, 49*(9), 12–13.

Moses, M. (2000). Future school executives: Who will be our leaders? *Texas School Business, 46* (8), 12–13.

Paige, R. (2001). Snapshot of a leader. *Insight, 15*(1), 26–31.

Patterson, J. (2000). *The anguish of leadership*. Arlington, VA: American Association of School Administrators.

Pierson, M., and Hall, R. (2001, May). Illinois School Superintendent Survey. *Illinois Association of School Administrators On-Line Publication*. Available online: www.iasaedu.org/publications/survey00-01.htm [accessed November 23, 2002].

Ramsey, K. (1997). Domestic relationships of the superintendency. *The School Administrator, 54*(2), 34–40.

Rohn, C. (2001). *Superintendent pool shallow? Perception or reality?* Paper presented at the annual conference of the National Council of Professors of Educational Administration, Houston, Texas, August 9, 2001.

Romm, T., and Mahler, S. (1986). A three-dimensional model for using case studies in the academic classroom. *Higher Education, 15*(6), 677–696.

Schon, D. (1987). *Educating the reflective practitioner*. San Francisco: Jossey-Bass.

Schwahn, C., and Spady, W. (1998). *Total leaders: Applying the best future-focuses change strategies to education*. Arlington, VA: American Association of School Administrators.

Short, P., and Scribner, J. (2000). *Case studies of the superintendency*. Lanham, MD: Scarecrow Press.

Shulman, L. S. (1996). Just in case: Reflections on learning from experience. In J. Colbert, P. Desbert, and K. Trimble (Eds.), *The case for education: Contemporary approaches for using case methods* (pp. 197–217). Needham Heights, MA: Allyn & Bacon.

Skrla, L. (2001, September 9). Textbook example of a gender gap. *Ft. Worth Star-Telegram*, 1F, 6F.

Standards for Advanced Programs in Educational Leadership for Principals, Superintendents, Curriculum Directors, and Supervisors. (2002). National Policy Board for Educational Administration. Available Online: www.ncate. org/ncate/staff.htm [accessed November 23, 2002].

Stoker, W. (1967). *The public school superintendency in Texas*. Unpublished doctoral dissertation, West Texas State University.

Storey, V. (2001). Dean, judge, and bishop: Lessons from a conflict and implications for school leaders. *International Electronic Journal for Leadership in Learning, 5*(17), 1–14. Available online: www.ucalgary.ca/~iejll/volume5/storey.html [accessed November 23, 2002].

Thompson, D., Wood, R., and Honeyman, D. (1994). *Fiscal leadership for schools*. White Plains, NY: Longman Publishing Group.

Wideen, M., Mayer-Smith, J., and Moon, B. (1998). A critical analysis of the research on learning to teach: Making the case for an ecological perspective on inquiry. *Review of Educational Research, 68*(2), 130–178.

Zemlicka, B. (2001). *The career paths of Texas public school superintendents*. Available online: www.texasisd.com [accessed November 23, 2002].

CHAPTER 1

A Memorial for Alyssa and Jenna

Texas Standard—Competency 001:

The superintendent knows how to act with integrity, with fairness, and in an ethical manner in order to promote the success of all students.

ISLLC Standard 5:

A school administrator is an educational leader who promotes the success of all students by acting with integrity, with fairness, and in an ethical manner.

NCATE Standard 5:

Candidates who complete the program are educational leaders who have the knowledge and ability to promote the success of all students by acting with integrity, with fairness, and in an ethical manner.

ABSTRACT

Two popular, admired high school seniors are killed in a car wreck. The family wants to memorialize them with a much-needed commons area for the high school that will contain a granite monument with a Christian message. The school superintendent feels the message does not pass the Lemon Test, and, therefore, is unacceptable. The entire community and the school board are against her decision. Is she wrong? Is there a way to reach consensus without antagonizing the grieving family, the school board, and the community and still follow the law?

---

*This case is a revised version of a case previously published. Lowery, S., and Harris, S. (2001 Winter). A memorial for Sarah and Alyssa. *The Journal of Cases in Educational Leadership, 4*(1). Available online: www.ucea.org/cases/index.html.

OBJECTIVES

Objective 1: The superintendent knows how to model and promote the highest standard of conduct, ethical principles, and integrity in decision making, actions, and behaviors.

Objective 2: The superintendent knows how to apply laws, policies, and procedures in a fair and reasonable manner.

Objective 3: The superintendent knows how to communicate effectively with all stakeholders.

Objective 4: The superintendent knows how to use effective consensus-building and conflict-management skills.

LITERATURE REVIEW

The role of the superintendent has undergone significant change in recent years. Today there is often more emphasis on curriculum and instruction, planning, and involving others in decision making than on managerial duties (Harris, Marshall, Lowery, and Buck, 2002). Yet Bennis (1997) emphasized that any leader who does not learn the importance of involving stakeholders, valuing their contributions, and utilizing the potential of human resources cannot be an effective leader.

Superintendents are also challenged with being community leaders who possess high moral values, honesty, and integrity. Schwahn and Spady (1998) connected these leadership components with the superintendents' ability to build cultural leadership based on integrity, commitment, and ability to be inclusive. At the same time, the superintendent must be well versed in the legality of school-based decisions. Consequently, the task of aligning all these qualities within a sound education so that the diverse groups within a community feel that their interests are met is a complex undertaking, at best (Owen and Ovando, 2000).

The Constitution of the United States and the constitutions of each of the states are sources of law under which public school systems operate. The First Amendment to the United States Constitution prohibits Congress from making laws that either respect establishment of religion or prohibit the free exercise of religion. The Establishment Clause is generally interpreted to mean that neither a state nor the federal government can set up a church. This wall of separation philosophy has been used since *Everson v. Board of Education,* 330 U.S. 1 (1947). Although the First Amendment speaks specifically about Congress, courts have found it to apply to local and state governments, including schools. Judges have interpreted this provision to 1) forbid the establishment of religion by the state and 2) guarantee free exercise of individual religious liberty (Zirkel, Richardson, and Goldberg, 1995).

An activity challenged as being in violation of the Establishment Clause will be found to be constitutional if it complies (answers in the affirmative to each of the questions) with the three-pronged test called the Lemon Test, a judicial test for determining when government practices violate the First Amendment clause (Fischer, Schimmel, and Kelly, 1999). The Lemon Test includes the following questions:

1. Is there a secular purpose?
2. Is the practice neutral, neither advancing nor inhibiting religion?
3. Is the government excessively entangled with religion?

A violation of any one of these tests will invalidate the practice. (See *Lemon v. Kurtzman,* 403 U.S. 602 (1971); *Lee v. Weisman,* 504 U.S. 577 (1992); *Jones v. Clear Creek I.S.D.,* 977 F.2d 963 (5th Cir. 1992); *Santa Fe I.S.D. v. Doe,* 120 S. Ct. 2266 (2000)).

Although the line between teaching about religion, which is permissible, and teaching religious tenets, which is clearly impermissible, is not entirely clear, public schools must adhere to Establishment Clause restrictions because students are captive audiences (Zirkel, Richardson and Goldberg, 1995).

In this case of religious neutrality, the U.S. Supreme Court overturned a Louisiana law requiring the teaching of creation science if evolution was taught. Families entrust public schools with the education of their children but condition their trust on the understanding that the classroom will not purposely be used to advance religious views that may conflict with the private beliefs of the student and his or her family. Students in such institutions are impressionable and their attendance is involuntary. (See *Edwards v. Aguillard,* 482 U.S. 578 (1987)).

A test of "subtle coercion" is appropriate for assessing challenges to public school practices under the Establishment Clause (Zirkel, Richardson, and Goldberg, 1995). In holding that school-sponsored, nondenominational prayers or benedictions at public school graduation exercises violated the Establishment Clause, the Court's majority found that the role of the school principal in planning, coordinating, and directing the ceremony created pervasive involvement on the part of public school officials and imposed social pressure on students to conform to religious orthodoxy. (See *Lee v. Weisman,* 504 U.S. 577 (1992)).

Whether a religious symbol, such as a cross or nativity scene, may be displayed in public schools depends on the circumstances of the case. The U.S. Supreme Court ruled that a nativity scene, a Santa Claus house, and a Christmas tree at a courthouse did not violate the Constitution. However, the U.S. Supreme Court also ruled that a nativity scene, displayed by itself on a courthouse lawn, did violate the Establishment Clause, but a menorah, standing outside the courthouse next to a Christmas tree and a sign about liberty, did not violate the Constitution (Zirkel, Richardson, and Goldberg, 1995). (See *County of Allegheny v. American Civil Liberties Union,* 492 U.S. 573 (1989)).

The courts have considered the content and context of the alleged religious display to determine whether a reasonable person would feel that the primary effect of the display is to advance or inhibit religion. For example, the use of "Blue Devil" as a school mascot was found to have a secular purpose and was allowed (McEllistrem, Grzywacz, and Roth, 2000). (See *Kunselman v. Western Reserve Local School District,* 70 F.3d 931 (6th Cir. 1995)). Additionally, courts have regarded permanent displays in public school buildings or grounds that depict religious themes as violating the Establishment Clause (McEllistrem, Grzywacz, and Roth, 2000). (See *Washigesic v. Bloomingdale Public Schools,* 83 F. Supp. 559 (W.D. Mich.1993)).

CASE STUDY

The School Board Meeting

Shiloh Independent School District (ISD) Superintendent Janna Holloway was the last person to leave the Shiloh ISD administration building on a beautiful summer night. She had waited until everyone else had left the parking lot before picking up her purse and keys to walk to her car. The board meeting had been a nightmare. She had been called un-Christian, un-American, uncaring, and several other accusations had been made that she had tried to block from her mind.

Recently Betsy and Warren Brooks had contacted Dr. Holloway about donating an outdoor commons area for Shiloh High School in memory of their daughter, Alyssa, and her friend, Jenna Eddings. In the center of this area they wanted to erect a large granite monument that would have references to born-again Christianity, belief in Jesus as Savior, and other elements of Southern Baptist theology. Dr. Holloway had recommended to the Shiloh ISD Board of Trustees that the commons area could be constructed only if all the references to Christianity were eliminated. The Shiloh ISD Board of Trustees had just voted 7-0 against her recommendation. Dr. Holloway had based her recommendation on the Lemon Test (*Lemon v. Kurtzman,* 1971).

Audience members, the largest group at any Shiloh ISD board meeting since Dr. Holloway had assumed the superintendency the previous summer, made encouraging remarks and murmurs of approval as board members denounced her recommendation that a specific theology should not be included on anything that would be placed on school property. Instead, they had approved the following message to be placed on the monument:

> *This area is dedicated in loving memory of Alyssa Brooks and Jenna Eddings. Alyssa, daughter of Betsy and Warren Brooks, and Jenna, daughter of Bob and Catherine Eddings, went to be with their Lord and Saviour, Jesus Christ, on November 29, 1999. Both Alyssa and Jenna had accepted Jesus as their saviour and served Him faithfully during their lives. They have both gone to Heaven to be with Him. Our prayer is that other students might accept Jesus through the testimony of their lives. Heaven's gain is our loss.*

Dr. Holloway had found the unkind comments made by members of the audience especially hurtful since she was also a member of the First Baptist Church in Shiloh, and the theology did reflect her personal beliefs. She had struggled with her recommendation that the proposed wording on the monument must be changed to something that was nonsectarian and would pass the widely used Lemon Test. She had visited with the church pastor and, although, he understood that the school district could not condone or advocate any specific theology, he still approved of the parents' choice of wording on the monument.

Who would have ever believed that the tragedy that began with the deaths of two popular high school seniors would spiral into an issue that threatened to divide the superintendent and the board? Who would have believed that this issue would open the school district to the possibility of legal sanctions and divide the constituents of the Shiloh ISD?

After all, the Shiloh ISD, which served nearly 4,000 students in a rural area in the heart of the Bible Belt, was mostly Protestant. There was only one Catholic parish, and it served a small congregation of Hispanic families. The local Southern Baptist, Methodist, and Presbyterian churches played important roles in the religious and social lives of the people.

Most of the families were either self-employed in the timber or logging business or worked at one of the local logging mills. However, nearly all families, as well as the staff of Shiloh ISD, reflected the values of prior generations in their fundamentalist thinking. There were never school activities scheduled for Wednesday evenings since most churches had mid-week religious services, and school activities on Sundays were unthinkable. Approximately 52 percent of the student body was white, 34 percent was African American, and the growing Hispanic population had almost reached 14 percent. Nearly 67 percent of the students of Shiloh ISD were eligible for free or reduced meals. There was no doubt that the schools and churches were the backbone of this rural, hard-working community.

The Beginning of the Story

At home Dr. Holloway's thoughts returned to the beginning of the story. The small community had been shocked and saddened by the untimely deaths of two popular senior girls in the late fall. The auto accident that had claimed both their young lives one icy night in November was a tragedy, and students, faculty members, and the entire community of Shiloh, Texas, had been stunned in their grief.

Jenna Eddings and Alyssa Brooks were cheerleaders, honor students, and leaders in a variety of school activities. Both girls had already been accepted to major state universities. Both were active in the First Baptist Church and held leadership positions in church youth programs. Jenna's scholarship to a nearby Baptist university had been based both on her academic record at Shiloh High School and on her years of leadership and service at the First Baptist Church. Jenna's parents, Bob and Catherine Eddings, were a middle-class couple with three younger children. Bob worked at the nearby power-generating plant in Yellowstone, Texas, and Catherine worked as a secretary for a local insurance agent. They were active in the community, participating in summer baseball and softball and in their church.

Alyssa's parents were both from influential Shiloh families. Alyssa's mother, Betsy Brooks, was a descendent of the early Texas hero Sam Houston, and she took pride in her many civic and community positions. Alyssa's father, Warren Brooks, was president of the Shiloh First National Bank. Alyssa had been their only child. The Brooks' wielded considerable influence in community and school affairs, but had always been reasonable people who worked for the common good.

In early February, when Betsy and Warren Brooks came to Dr. Holloway with a proposal to donate funds for construction of an outdoor commons area at Shiloh High School in memory of their daughter and Jenna Eddings, Dr. Holloway was enthusiastic and offered to help in any way that she could. The proposed commons area would include a paved area with picnic tables, benches, and other seating arrangements, landscaping, and a granite monument. The outside commons area for students was badly needed and would make a wonderful gathering place for high school students. Dr. Holloway suggested that board approval for the donation would most likely be readily granted.

Mr. and Mrs. Brooks would be donating most of the funding, with some assistance from Jenna's parents. The youth group at First Baptist Church had held car washes and other fund-raisers to make a contribution to the project.

Dr. Holloway placed acceptance of the donation as an action item at the June board meeting. She felt so confident in the proposal after talking with Mr. and Mrs. Brooks that she did not actually view the plans until two weeks before the board meeting. When local architect Lance Thompson brought the plans to her office for inclusion in the packet of materials being distributed to board members in preparation for the June board meeting, she read the message that was to be inscribed on the monument for the first time. When she voiced her concerns to Mr. Thompson, he pointed out that almost everyone in Shiloh belonged to one of the Protestant churches and that the message would surely not offend anyone. Mr. Thompson, chairman of the Board of Deacons at First Baptist Church, was surprised that she felt the message inappropriate for the high school.

After Mr. Thompson left her office, Dr. Holloway immediately took the plans and went downtown to the bank to talk with Warren Brooks. What a situation! How would she tell this grieving parent that the memorial so lovingly proposed for his daughter and her best friend was not appropriate for a public school? How could she put into words the conflict between her personal religious conviction and the need for religious neutrality in a public school?

Warren Brooks listened to her carefully and then asserted his position. The monument would be inscribed with the message contained in the set of plans. There would be no changes. He and his wife had met with Jenna's parents, and the two couples had written the message carefully, reflecting their daughters' convictions. His thoughts were in line with those of the architect: who could object to such a message of hope and love? The message was certainly in accord with the theology of the major churches in Shiloh.

Dr. Holloway visited with Bob and Catherine Eddings that same night, and their position was the same as that voiced by Warren Brooks. The message was crucial. It was one that their daughters would have wanted.

The Superintendent's Recommendation

When Dr. Holloway met with board president Meredith Johnson to review the board agenda, she described the dilemma and explained why she could not recommend that the board approve the construction. Mrs. Johnson disagreed with her emphatically and informed her that she was sure the rest of the board would vote to reject her recommendation also. After all, the commons was needed; the families were strong supporters of the school; and this was a Christian community. The monument would be built, and the message would stay as proposed.

DISCUSSION TOPICS/QUESTIONS

1. Consider each of the law cases mentioned and discuss their effect on Shiloh ISD.
2. Should Dr. Holloway have gone immediately to the parents when she realized that the proposed message on the monument might be a problem?
3. What suggestions would you make for Dr. Holloway to engage the parents in writing a message that would be acceptable when placed on school property?
4. What might Dr. Holloway have done to gain support from the board?
5. Is there a way that the pastor might have been able to support the grieving families and also to support Dr. Holloway in this difficult decision?
6. Since "everyone" in the community belongs to one of the Protestant churches anyway, what difference will it make to erect this monument with the Christian message?
7. What are your predictions regarding Dr. Holloway's long-term success as superintendent? Support your answer.
8. In what way might superintendent board training have avoided this situation?
9. How can Dr. Holloway regain the support of the community, the board, and the Brooks and the Eddings?
10. Write a message that might satisfy the grieving parents and also satisfy the Lemon Test.

REFERENCES

Bennis, W. (1997). *Managing people is like herding cats.* Provo, UT: Executive Excellence Publishing.

County of Allegheny v. American Civil Liberties Union, 492 U.S. 573 (1989).

Edwards v. Aguillard, 482 U.S. 578 (1987).

Everson v. Board of Education, 330 U.S. 1 (1947).

Fischer, L., Schimmel, D., and Kelly, C. (1999). *Teachers and the law* (5th ed.). New York: Addison Wesley Longman.

Harris, S., Marshall, R., Lowery, S., and Buck, J. (2002). Community input into a selection of a superintendent. *Education Leadership Review*, *3*(2), 22–27.

Jones v. Clear Creek I.S.D., 977 F.2d 963 (5th Cir. 1992).

Kunselman v. Western Reserve Local School District, 70 F.3d 931 (6th Cir. 1995).

Lee v. Weisman, 504 U.S. 577 (1992).

Lemon v. Kurtzman, 403 U.S. 602 (1971).

McEllistrem, S., Grzywacz, P., and Roth, J. A., eds. (2000). *Deskbook encyclopedia of American school law*. Burnsville, MN: Oakstone Legal & Business Publishing.

Owen, J., and Ovando, M. (2000). *Superintendent's guide to creating community*. Lanham, MD: Scarecrow Press.

Santa Fe I.S.D. v. Doe, 120 S. Ct. 2266 (2000).

Schwahn, C., and Spady, W. (1998). Total leaders: Applying the best future-focuses change strategies to education. *Education Week on the Web, 18*(38), 32, 44. Available online: www.edweek.org [accessed February 2000].

Washigesic v. Bloomingdale Public Schools, 813 F. Supp. 559 (W.D. Mich. 1993).

Zirkel, P., Richardson, S. N., and Goldberg, S. S. (1995). *A digest of Supreme Court decisions effecting education* (3rd ed.). Bloomington, IN: Phi Delta Kappa Educational Foundation.

ADDITIONAL RESOURCES

Alexander, K., and Alexander, M. David. (1998). *American public school law* (4th ed.). Belmont, CA: Wadsworth Publishing Company.

La Morte, M. W. (2002). *School law: Cases and concepts* (7th ed.). Boston: Allyn & Bacon.

Mawdsley, R. D. (1999). Religious activities in public schools. *NASSP Bulletin, 83*(610), 8–13.

CHAPTER 2

A Culture of Success or the Emperor's New Clothes?

Texas Standard—Competency 002:

The superintendent knows how to shape district culture by facilitating the development, articulation, implementation, and stewardship of a vision of learning that is shared and supported by the educational community.

ISLLC Standard 1:

A school administrator is an educational leader who promotes the success of all students by facilitating the development, articulation, implementation, and stewardship of a vision of learning that is shared and supported by the school community.

NCATE Standard 1:

Candidates who complete the program are educational leaders who have the knowledge and ability to promote the success of all students by facilitating the development, articulation, implementation, and stewardship of a school or district vision of learning supported by the school community.

ABSTRACT

The community newspaper editorial is extremely critical of the school superintendent Dr. Susan Wilkins. When she took the job two years earlier, she predicted that the school district would move forward dramatically with her education reforms. But just the opposite has happened. How can she articulate her vision into a vision shared by the community and work with stakeholders to bring about positive school reform?

OBJECTIVES

Objective 1: The superintendent is able to establish a culture that promotes learning, high expectations, and academic rigor for
students, staff, and community advocacy groups.

Objective 2: The superintendent is able to facilitate the development and
implementation of a shared vision to ensure student success.

Objective 3: The superintendent is able to collaborate with family and
community in policy development, program planning,
and assessment processes.

Objective 4: The superintendent is able to maintain awareness of emerging issues and trends affecting education and communicate
their significance to the local educational community.

LITERATURE REVIEW

An important attribute of educational leadership is visionary ability. In
fact, Max DePree (1990) describes a major responsibility of a leader as
that of defining reality for the organization. In other words, the superintendent must be able to evaluate the status of a school district and dis-
cern educational possibilities (Owen and Ovando, 2000). However, a
vision must result in goal orientation that implements strategies to improve teaching and learning. Congruent with this, Holdaway and
Genge (1995) report that educational leaders must be action oriented as
well as be able to delegate effectively.

At the core of successful school leadership is the ability to develop a
positive organizational culture. Leaders must understand the nuances
of change—external and internal forces that affect change (Calabrese,
2002). One model to implement is the Four Cornerstones of Successful
School Change, which includes:

1. Culture of Success—encourage high expectations and support students in achievement at high levels;
2. Capacity-Building—focus all professional development on goals
and purposes of the schools;
3. Systems Thinking—recognize that all elements in the system are
connected as part of a larger system;

4. Leadership for Success—exercise transformational leadership and allocate more time to advance the school vision. (Reavis, Vinson, and Fox, 1999; Leifeste, 2001)

Another concern for superintendents is the "degree of centralization or decentralization to be maintained in the district regarding curriculum and instruction" (Owen and Ovando, 2000, p. 82). Years ago, superintendents held positions of power that frequently allowed them to set the agenda and make decisions with little input from other groups. However, in the twenty-first century, diverse community coalitions often mandate that educational decisions be made in response to current political conditions.

At the same time, superintendents generally value when school problems are "resolved at the school level and when external resources are secured with little encumbrance to the district" (Glascock and Taylor, 2001, p. 2). This often leads to site-based decision making, which promotes leadership that "comes from both ends" (Schmoker, 2001, p. 94).

This process of widening the circle of involvement involves principals, teachers, parents, students and other community members in shared decision making. In fact, even when very few agree on anything, just having "access to information, involvement and influence" leads to ownership of the plan (p. 94). Therefore, superintendents must be actively involved in collecting information about the educational community that includes customs and traditions, population characteristics, communication channels, community groups, leadership, economic conditions, political structure, social tensions, and previous community efforts (Bagin and Gallagher, 2001).

Additionally, superintendents must be aware of the power of the press and its ability to influence public opinion. In fact, according to Kaplan (1992), how could any journalist resist the opportunity to tell education's story when the success of our 105,000 schools, 46 million students, over 2 million teachers, and 15,500 school districts is such a massive endeavor? Thus, superintendents must actively work to improve public confidence in the educational system. Some of these strategies include 1) informing the public about successes and challenges; 2) taking the public's concern about school issues seriously; 3) personalizing the schools; 4) improving staff morale; 5) building coalitions; 6) working with the business community; 7) involving parents and nonparents in the school; and 8) recognizing that the communications program is a two-way process (Bagin and Gallagher, 2001).

CASE STUDY

The Editorial

Ashcroft Independent School District (ISD) Superintendent Dr. Susan Wilkins read the following editorial in the *Ashcroft Daily Journal* this morning. Although she knew that her support was wavering, she had not really expected the strength of the editorial.

Leadership Crisis in the Ashcroft ISD

While preliminary results indicate that students across the state scored well on the State Assessment of Academic Skills (SAAS) test this year, that is not the case for Ashcroft ISD students. In a written statement provided to the Ashcroft Daily Journal before Tuesday night's school board meeting, Dr. Susan Wilkins said the overall district results are a disappointment and that they do not meet either the district expectations or the goals set by the board of trustees.

Dr. Wilkins took responsibility for the district's performance on the test results and will take action to determine why reform efforts, such as designing new curriculum, professional development, and employing new personnel have not been more successful. Dr. Wilkins noted that the district's performance on the SAAS diminished achievements in other areas. Although Dr. Wilkins stepped forward to take responsibility for the district's poor performance on the tests of reading, language arts, mathematics, social studies, and science, it is unacceptable that our students scored so far below the state averages. Two of the district's fourteen campuses will be rated "Low Performing" based on these test scores. Twenty-two seniors will be excluded from graduation ceremonies on May 25 because they have yet to pass all three sections of the exit-level State Assessment of Academic Skills.

When Dr. Susan Wilkins accepted the superintendency two years ago, she predicted that the Ashcroft ISD would achieve the state's highest level of accreditation status in two years. What has happened is just the opposite. Teacher morale and student morale are at all time lows, the district's accreditation status has not improved, board members are at odds due to personnel issues, yet district spending on a per-pupil basis is greater than similar school districts.

Is it time for the school board to confront Dr. Wilkins about her leadership and her failure to make good on promises? Has her mantra about building a culture of success actually been a case of the emperor's new clothes, with everyone reluctant to speak the truth?

Creating a Culture of Success

When Dr. Wilkins accepted the Ashcroft ISD superintendency two years earlier, she already had one very successful superintendency on her resume. She was exactly what the Ashcroft ISD Board of Trustees wanted: a superintendent with new ideas, an aggressive leadership style, and a willingness to tackle old paradigms. During her first few months as Ashcroft ISD superintendent, she had predicted that the district was ready to move to the next century, and she was ready to provide the leadership necessary for a successful journey. Her commitment to academic success for all students was the district's new theme.

She was described by her supporters as a no-nonsense leader who was willing to support innovative campus administrators but who expected results. "She's tough, but fair," was a frequently heard description of Dr. Wilkins. Indeed, she would have described her leadership style in similar terms. She had shared her thoughts on student achievement with parent, civic, and other community groups on numerous occasions, "Educators long ago adopted the philosophy that all children can learn. In this school district, we will put that philosophy into practice. We've set high expectations and our educators and children will work hard to achieve these expectations."

Her critics had been heard to describe her as "ruthless." One former Ashcroft ISD principal said, "She takes no prisoners and leaves no wounded." Another was on record as saying, "She talks a good game, but it's all talk. Basically, it's her way or the highway."

The school board had supported her recommendations and the strong measures she had recommended. During her first year with the Ashcroft ISD, she had required every teacher and administrator to participate in extra days of professional development. Faculty and staff members received extra compensation for those days, and nationally known consultants were brought to Ashcroft to lead the sessions.

During her first year as Ashcroft ISD superintendent, she had appointed a small cadre of leaders on each campus to work with her and other central office leaders to achieve change. The old practices of "good enough" and "that's the way we've always done things" were no longer satisfactory if every student was going to be successful. She had reassigned nine of the district's fourteen principals at the end of her second year because they had not moved quickly enough to implement the new district vision of academic success,. The school board had supported this controversial move, in spite of considerable community opposition. Six of the nine reassigned principals had retired, one had found employment in a nearby school district, and the other two accepted new assignments in other administrative positions.

New principals were selected from outside the district, and an extensive curriculum alignment project had been started. Class sizes were reduced on all elementary campuses, lowering the pupil-teacher ratio to 1 to 22 in grades kindergarten through five throughout the district.

Low-Performing Campuses and Seniors Who Did Not Make the Grade

Now at the end of Dr. Wilkins' second year, teacher morale was low and two new school board members who openly opposed her ideas had been elected the previous month. When State Assessment of Academic Skills (SAAS) scores arrived from the State Education Agency the previous week, she and other Ashcroft ISD educators were devastated. SAAS scores in many areas were significantly lower than state averages.

Two campuses, Willowbrook Elementary and Ashcroft High School, were designated Low-Performing Campuses by the State Education Agency. This designation meant that both campuses would be reviewed by State Education Agency Review Teams the following year. These teams of educators, working with Ashcroft ISD leadership, would have the responsibility of assessing current educational programs and making recommendations for improvement. No superintendent would take this situation lightly, and Dr. Wilkins was very aware of the implications for the Ashcroft ISD.

When several of the nongraduating seniors and Ashcroft High School principal Deborah Black were interviewed by the local television station the previous Saturday evening, the story revealed a human side to the SAAS crisis. "If seniors don't pass the exam, state law prohibits them from getting a diploma. The exit test is first given at the sophomore level, and students who fail it have seven other opportunities to take the test before the end of their senior year," Black told reporters.

Ashcroft High School senior Justin Muench said he did not know the consequences of the SAAS until he failed the mathematics and writing sections as a sophomore. He passed the writing section during his junior year, but has been unsuccessful on the mathematics portion of the test. "I didn't know you couldn't graduate," said Muench. "The first time, I took it like nothing. When I found out I needed it to graduate, I tried harder."

A Culture of Success or the Emperor's New Clothes?

Dr. Wilkins was preparing to meet with her leadership team, the assistant superintendents, and other central office administrators who would have responsibilities for explaining the test scores at the school board meeting the following week. She knew her goals were right for this district. Her leadership team and her school board had supported her efforts. What was wrong? How could things be turned around for the children of Ashcroft ISD.

DISCUSSION TOPICS/QUESTIONS

1. If you were Dr. Wilkins, what would be your first action in response to the editorial?
2. How would you discuss this with the district leadership team?
3. Identify the leadership style that appears to characterize Dr. Wilkins' actions. What recommendations would you make to her regarding leadership? Support your recommendations.
4. What processes could be used to gather data assessing the climate among the faculty and community?

5. Construct a sample survey to gather data from faculty regarding their commitment to the school's academic vision.

6. Using force-field analysis or another specific strategy of your own choosing, identify barriers to Dr. Wilkins' plan for the district. Identify positive aspects of her plan for the district.

7. Based on the information gathered in question 6, what steps would you recommend that Dr. Wilkins follow to help Ashcroft ISD truly implement the vision of learning for all students?

8. Construct a plan for working with the media in this case study. Extend it to your own district.

9. What ideas would you suggest to change the current negative attitude of the community toward the education in this district?

10. Using the information from this case, how might you rewrite the editorial to report the news but still support the superintendent and her efforts for reform?

11. Are two years sufficient to turn around a district? Explain your answer, citing several sources from current literature.

REFERENCES

Bagin, D., and Gallagher, D. (2001). *The school and community relations* (7th ed.). Boston: Allyn & Bacon.

Calabrese, R. (2002). *The leadership assignment: Creating change.* Boston: Allyn & Bacon.

DePree, M. (1990). *Leadership is an art.* New York: Dell Press.

Glascock, C., and Taylor, D. (2001). The elementary principal/superintendent relationship as perceived by teachers and its effects on the school: A case study comparison. *Education Policy Analysis Archives, 9*(45). Available online: http://epaa.asu.edu/epaa/v9n45.html [accessed October 31, 2001].

Holdaway, E., and Genge, A., (1995). How effective superintendents understand their own work. In *Effective school district leadership: Transforming politics into education* (50–58). Ed. K. Leithwood. New York: State University of New York Press.

Kaplan, G. R. (1992). *Images of education: The mass media's version of America's schools.* Washington, DC: Institute for Educational Leadership.

Leifeste, K. F. (2001). *Preparing your school for success: Initiating culture improvement through level I changes.* Paper presented at the National Council for Professors of Educational Administration annual meeting, August 7, 2001, Houston, Texas.

Owen, J., and Ovando, M. (2000). *Superintendent's guide to creating community.* Lanham, MD: Scarecrow Press.

Reavis, C. A., Vinson, D., and Fox, R. (1999). Importing a culture of success via a strong principal. *The Clearing House, 72*(4), 199–202.

Schmoker, M. (2001). *The results fieldbook.* Alexandria, VA: Association for Supervision and Curriculum Development.

ADDITIONAL RESOURCES

Brown, D. (1991). *Decentralization: The administrator's guidebook to school district change.* Newbury Park, CA: Corwin.

Covey, S. (1991). *The seven habits of highly effective people.* New York: Simon & Schuster.

Fullan, M., and Hargreaves, A. (1996). *What's worth fighting for in your school?* New York: Teachers College Press.

Lambert, L. (1998). *Building leadership capacity in schools.* Alexandria, VA: Association for Supervision and Curriculum Development.

Short, P., and Scribner, J. P., eds. (2000). *Case studies of the superintendency.* Lanham, MD: The Scarecrow Press.

CHAPTER 3

The Blytheville Story: The Challenge of Changing Demographics

Texas Standard—Competency 003:
  The superintendent knows how to communicate and collaborate with
  families and community members, respond to diverse community interests and needs, and mobilize community resources to ensure educational success for all students.

ISLLC Standard 4:
  A school administrator is an educational leader who promotes the
  success of all students by collaborating with families and community
  members, responding to diverse community interests and needs, and
  mobilizing community resources.

NCATE 4:
  Candidates who complete the program are educational leaders who
  have the knowledge and ability to promote the success of all students
  by collaborating with families and other community members, responding to diverse community interests and needs, and mobilizing
  community resources.

ABSTRACT

The superintendency of a public school system is an increasingly
complex position that has been described as a focal point for any dis-
content with the schools. Regardless of the size of the school district,

---

*This case is a version of a case previously published. Lowery, S., & Harris, S. (2002, Fall). The
Blytheville story: The challenge of changing demographics. *The Journal of Cases in Educational
Leadership, 5*(3). Available: www.ucea.org/cases/index.html.

the superintendent of schools bears the responsibility for leading schools that are devoted to students, exemplified by decisions that reflect learner-centered values. This case describes a community that was changing rapidly: demographically, politically, and philosophically. Superintendents and board relationships were challenged to overcome discord and begin to communicate a united community ideology.

OBJECTIVES

Objective 1: The superintendent promotes the success of all students by collaborating with families and community members.
Objective 2: The superintendent promotes the success of all students by responding to diverse community interests and needs.
Objective 3: The superintendent promotes the success of all students by mobilizing community resources.

LITERATURE REVIEW

In every community, there are many external influences that have strong effects on the local school system. These influences can come from parents, political and legal patterns, and demographic characteristics, to name just a few (Hoy and Miskel, 2001). Because of these changing demographics, the growing diversity of communities, and other external influences, the role of the superintendent is faced with even greater challenges in the twenty-first century (Kowalski, 1999). Organizational health is most effective when the schools mirror the norms, values, and philosophies of the surrounding society (Rowan, 1993). However, for a school to mirror the community surrounding it, the leader must first have a clear understanding of that community.

Other essential leadership steps that transform schools include creating a clear vision for the school, developing a strategy to accomplish this vision, and communicating effectively with all stakeholders (Yukl, 1998). Schools cannot transform themselves, therefore, when school improvement efforts are needed and the broader administrative, social, and political environment must be considered (Sergiovanni, 2001). In fact, effective change is largely influenced by the political community, attitudes of teachers, the school board, and the administration (Kirst, 1984). Because of the many stakeholders involved, successful leadership recognizes and cultivates collaborative leadership within these diverse groups (Lambert, 1998; Sergiovanni, 1992). Still, one of the most powerful advocates to transform a school district is the superintendent working with the support of the school board and the community (Fullan, 1993).

Successful schools are built when there is a link between the school "being able to develop social capital for all its students" (Sergiovanni, 2001, p. 177) and the student's engagement with the school. Schools develop social capital by being caring communities (Sergiovanni, 2001), which leads to a sense of community that binds everyone to a shared ideology (Pellicer, 1999; Sergiovanni, 2001).

The superintendent must be a great communicator of this ideology, as well as a great persuader, especially when working with the local school board (Houston, 2001). In fact, just as in the Blytheville ISD, the "disconnect" between superintendents, school boards, and the community can result in years of dysfunction and student suffering. Healing can only come when school leaders care enough about the larger community to address issues of diversity, recognize the political climate of the community, and communicate a shared ideology. Ultimately, ideologies influence what we believe and what we do and tie people together to commit themselves to a course of action (Sergiovanni, 2001), which, hopefully, will result in a school district that is focused on students as learners.

CASE STUDY

An Era of Change

Blytheville Independent School District (ISD), a suburban school district in central Texas, had changed in the last ten years from a small, rural district that served one farming and ranching community to a mid-size district of 8,350 students. Blytheville is an old community with settlement history dating back to the 1840s, during the Republic of Texas. Until the population changes of the mid-1980s, the community had remained rural in its perspective, with strong farming and ranching influences. The school district had also remained rural in its perspective, with a basic curriculum that emphasized vocational training, strong interest in athletics, and a conservative approach to business affairs. While parental interest and support for the schools were evident, the superintendent and school board ran the school, and few individuals voiced challenges to the "way we have always done things."

However, changes began in the mid-1980s with the development of the Azure Bay Subdivision, a gated community of expensive homes with excellent golf and tennis facilities located on Lake Central Texas. The homes sold rapidly, and the subdivision was soon home to many young professionals and retired professionals, including several physicians and attorneys.

Many Azure Bay residents did not have children in school, and while they were certainly advocates of a strong, effective public school system, they were not actively involved in Blytheville ISD affairs. Those young professionals with children were concerned about the lack of college-preparatory courses and that there was no gifted and talented program within the district. Azure Bay, along with two other similar gated subdivisions on Lake East Texas, added a distinctly different population to the original community of Blytheville.

Another population dimension was added when two mobile home subdivisions opened on Lake Central Texas. Many of the families who moved into these homes spoke primarily Spanish and brought significant numbers of low socioeconomic children into the district. This necessitated the involvement of public health and social service agencies. These families were not hesitant to voice their expectations about how their children should be served.

Because these subdivisions were on property that had originally been the Bar T Ranch, this part of the school district came to be known as the Taylorville area, since the Taylor family had owned the Bar T Ranch. This newest group was the fastest growing of any population group and was characterized by high mobility, substandard housing, and high unemployment. The children from this group brought personal and educational needs to Blytheville ISD that often challenged the old ways of doing things.

In one decade, Blytheville ISD had changed from a district composed of one rural, homogeneous community to a community serving four diverse populations: old rural Blytheville; the upscale Azure Bay

THE BLYTHEVILLE STORY   25

area of retirees without children; young, well-educated professionals; and the low socioeconomic Taylorville area. These separate, very diverse communities, with new residents and new ideas, caused rapid change in the Blytheville ISD.

Educational Leadership in an Era of Change

Mike Warren had been superintendent several years when the population growth began. Soon every building was crowded, and there was an acute need for additional facilities. The district was able to pass a bond issue, and a new high school complex was built. By the time the high school was completed, more facilities were needed. Since the bond issue had funded a high school building complete with gymnasium, band hall, facilities for career and technology classes, stadium, field house, and auditorium, there was considerable opposition to another bond issue so soon. The school board voted to call an election for a second bond issue and the matter was presented to voters. The bond issue would have raised local taxes above the state average, and many residents voted against the second bond issue, causing the issue to fail.

Along with the failure of the bond issue, the overcrowding problems, and the sociological changes in the student population, changes in the composition of the school board eventually led to Warren's resignation. The new board included several members who wanted rapid change and felt that Warren was not the superintendent to lead the district at that time.

Three board members were very vocal and felt that a more involved school board was needed. They ardently challenged the district's attention to athletics and its lack of emphasis on academics. These particular board members openly engaged in micromanagement, involving themselves in administrative functions that were outside their responsibilities as board members. These board members called for Warren's resignation, censuring him for clinging to old outdated concepts of school administration and urging an end to "the good old boy network."

During the next few years, the Blytheville ISD continued to grow, with new subdivisions opening regularly. Warren did resign, but his successor stayed in office only eighteen months. The school board's dysfunctional intervention into the day-to-day management of the school district continued, and the Blytheville ISD gained the reputation of a revolving door for administrators, with five new superintendents and three new principals in seven years. As the struggles between administrators and the board members intensified, teacher morale worsened and there was little interest in academic improvement. Gossip seemed to be the main industry of the school, and the illness of the school district soon spread into several of the churches and the small city government. One longtime resident commented, "We've got our business in a mess. We need someone to step in and straighten out our school."

Confronting the Issues

Finally, the separate communities that composed the Blytheville ISD began to recognize the seriousness of the school district's malaise. Three new board members were elected, unseating three of the most contentious board members. Shortly after reorganization of the board following the election, the board voted unanimously to contact the State Education Agency and ask for help with their governance problems. The State Education Agency responded to their request and assigned a "master" to head the district. The designation of a master gave complete control to this state-designated individual to run the district. In fact, this individual's power superceded that of the school board.

The master, retired superintendent James Hazelwood, worked as Blytheville ISD interim superintendent for eight months. Although his role as master allowed him total control over all aspects of the district, including all school board decisions, he began to work with the board and community in a quiet, professional manner. Dr. Hazlewood was an experienced administrator with a thorough understanding of school finance, school law, and administrative practices, and he was also totally committed to students. During the early stages of his work at Blytheville ISD, he frequently told the board, "We can defend a decision that's best for kids. We can't defend political decisions."

Soon after taking over, Dr. Hazlewood focused new board training on understanding the community and how it was changing, and then he began to work with them in identifying a shared vision for the community's schools. Dr. Hazlewood quickly became involved in the local community and spoke at several civic meetings, as well as at local churches. He always centered his topic on the students within the community and their need to be equipped educationally. Gradually, the board began to consider his recommendations without the hostility that had divided previous boards.

Reconstruction of a School District

Since Dr. Hazelwood's role was by legislative mandate, that of an interim, a new superintendent was selected. The school board hired Dr. David Bruce, a beginning superintendent with successful experience as a campus administrator in a neighboring school district. The community diversity and strife became immediately obvious when Dr. Bruce held his first community meeting. He looked out over the crowd and noticed that there were clearly, at least, four factions in the room with one empty row separating each group. Young, professional men and women sat together toward the front, looking comfortable and well-dressed; just behind them sat a row of casually dressed older men and women. Over to the left, a group clustered around a local pastor, and he knew that this was the rural "old guard" who had been educated in this very Blytheville school. Sitting toward the back, looking watchful and guarded, was a group of young and old families, mostly women. Dr. Bruce knew that these people were from the Taylorville community and were relatively new to the district. School faculty, and even some students, sat by themselves in other areas of the room. It was obvious that the years of strife had left many divisions within the community. What could he do to bring a sense of one community to these very different groups?

DISCUSSION TOPICS/QUESTIONS

1. Discuss the impact on a school district of a changing community population.
2. Identify strategies that a school district should have in place to address changing diversity of its population. How might this have diminished the conflict within this case study?
3. What external factors affect a school other than diversity of population?

4. Why should the school district consider external factors in its planning?

5. Based on general knowledge about leadership styles, what role might leadership have had in the contentious relationships of these superintendents and the school board?

6. Why does collaborative leadership appear to be most productive in this school district for bringing about positive change?

7. Design a plan for the superintendent to implement that will involve the local media in a positive way in this situation.

8. Identify strategies for developing and implementing the concept of "social capacity" within diverse school communities that builds learner-centered schools.

9. Suggest ways that a university superintendent or principal preparation program could better prepare students to incorporate the practice of collaborative leadership.

REFERENCES

Fullan, M. (1993). *Change forces.* London, U.K.: Falmer Press.

Houston, P. (2001). Superintendents for the 21st century: It's not just a job, it's a calling. *Educational Leadership, 82*(6), 429–433.

Hoy, W., and Miskel, C. (2001). *Educational administration: Theory, research, and practice* (6th ed.). Boston: McGraw Hill.

Kirst, M. (1984). *Who controls our schools?* New York: Freeman.

Kowalski, T. (1999). *The school superintendent: Theory, practice, and cases.* Upper Saddle River, NJ: Prentice Hall.

Lambert, L. (1998). How to build leadership capacity. *Educational Leadership, 55*(7), 17–19.

Pellicer, L. (1999). *Caring enough to lead: Schools and the sacred trust.* Thousand Oaks, CA: Corwin Press.

Rowan, B. (1993, February). *Institutional studies of organization: Lines of analysis and data requirements.* Paper presented at the annual meeting of the American Educational Research Association, Atlanta, GA.

Sergiovanni, T. (1992). *Moral leadership: Getting to the heart of school improvement.* San Francisco: Jossey-Bass.

Sergiovanni, T. (2001). *The principalship: A reflective practice perspective* (4th ed.). Boston: Allyn & Bacon.

Yukl, G. (1998). *Leadership in organizations* (4th ed.). Upper Saddle River, NJ: Prentice Hall.

ADDITIONAL RESOURCES

Bridges, W. (1991). *Managing transitions: Making the most of change*. Reading, MA: Addison Wesley.

Johnson, S. M. (1996). *Leading to change: The challenge of the new superintendency*. San Francisco: Jossey-Bass.

Lowery, S. (2001). Standards for Texas school board members. In *Schooling and standards in the US: An encyclopedia*. Ed. J. Kincheloe, S. Steinberg, and D. Weil. Santa Barbara, CA: ABC-CLO.

Lowery, S., Harris, S., and Marshall, R. (2002). Hiring a superintendent: Public relations challenge. *Journal of School Public Relations, 23*(1), 70–79.

Lowery, S., McNaughten, D., and Zachary, F. (1998). Roles and responsibilities of the superintendent and board of trustees in a learner-centered community. *Journal of the Effective Schools Project (4)*.

Norton, M., Webb, L., Dlugosh, L., and Sybouts, W. (1996). *The school superintendency: New responsibilities, new leadership*. Boston, MA: Allyn & Bacon.

Owen, J., and Ovando, M. (2000). *Superintendent's guide to creating community*. Lanham, MD: Scarecrow Press.

Palestini, R. (1999). *Educational administration: Leading with mind and heart*. Lancaster, PA: Technomic.

Sergiovanni, T. (2000). *The lifeworld of leadership: Creating culture, community and personal meaning in our schools*. San Francisco: Jossey-Bass.

Valdez, A., Milstein, M., Wood, C., and Jacquez, D. (1999). *How to turn a school around: What principals can do*. Thousand Oaks, CA: Corwin Press.

CHAPTER 4

The Politics of School Reform

Texas Standard—Competency 004:
> The superintendent knows how to respond to and influence the larger political, social, economic, legal, and cultural context, including working with the board of trustees, to achieve the district's educational vision.

ISLLC Standard 6:
> A school administrator is an educational leader who promotes the success of all students by understanding, responding to, and influencing the larger political, social, economic, legal, and cultural context.

NCATE Standard 6:
> Candidates who complete the program are educational leaders who have the knowledge and ability to promote the success of all students by understanding, responding to, and influencing the larger political, social, economic, legal, and cultural context.

ABSTRACT

A major responsibility for any school superintendent is to work within the political framework of the school board and the community. The ability to influence district constituents toward implementing appropriate school reform components is necessary for continued success. This case describes a superintendent with a school board that has changed substantially since his employment. He still believes in a vision of what is best for students, but the challenge is in accomplishing this objective.

OBJECTIVES

Objective 1: The superintendent knows how to analyze and respond to political, social, economic, and cultural factors affecting students and education.

Objective 2: The superintendent knows how to work with the board of trustees to define mutual expectations, policies, and standards.

Objective 3: The superintendent knows how to communicate and work effectively with board members in varied contexts, including problem-solving and decision-making contexts.

Objective 4: The superintendent knows how to prepare and recommend district policies to improve student learning and district performance in compliance with state and federal requirements.

LITERATURE REVIEW

The role of the superintendent is a changing dynamic. According to Murphy (2001), in the early part of the twentieth century, generally, the technical and mechanical aspects of administration were emphasized. In the years between 1950 and 1985, the conceptual and theoretical knowledge base of the superintendency began to move toward a foundation of scientifically supported knowledge to inform practice. However, in the new millennium, the role of the superintendent is much broader than ever before and encompasses knowledge of "transformational and change dynamics," "an appreciation of the collegial and collaborative foundations," as well as a clear "emphasis on the ethical and reflective dimensions of leadership" (Murphy, 2001, p. 15).

Still, it is the role of the superintendent to work with the board in achieving the district's educational vision. Yet a positive working relationship with the school board is ranked as the number one challenge that superintendents face. Clearly this is not an easy task as evidenced by a recent survey conducted by Thomas Glass at the University of Memphis that found that 64 percent of 175 high-performing superintendents classified "their relationships with their boards as poor" (Sternberg, 2002, p. 13). Another study reported that 81 percent of superintendents believe that talented administrators leave education because they are frustrated by difficult pressures of the politics that surround this job (Farkas, Johnson, Duffett, and Foleno, 2001).

While conflict is a natural part of the superintendency, considering all of the stakeholders with whom this role operates, it clearly affects every aspect of the organization. Generally, conflict is influenced by place, issues, and people involved (Owen and Ovando, 2000). Yet all too frequently, school leaders find themselves ill equipped to resolve conflicts (Storey, 2001). Still, there are knowledge and skills to be considered that can strengthen a superintendent's ability to successfully bring about resolution in the variety of settings in which conflict occurs. Chief among these skills are human relations behaviors that communicate to others a positive attitude toward the "supreme worth of all individuals" (Bagin and Gallagher, 2001, p. 91).

Therefore, in order to resolve conflict effectively, the superintendent must foster a spirit of collegiality and good will among every level of the school system. The superintendent must be aware of the importance of communicating in actions, not just words, and be sensitive to staff perceptions of decision making. Additionally, superintendent leadership that fosters unity among staff will decrease occurrences of conflict by bringing staff together to share ideas, to define instructional issues, to pool resources, to identify appropriate goals, and to collaborate on implementation of objectives (Bagin and Gallagher, 2001).

One strategy for reducing conflict and increasing staff agreement is to implement the concept of quality circles. This process involves six primary steps: problem identification, problem selection, problem analysis, recommended solutions, management review, and recommendations for implementation. This process improves better communications in a variety of ways, such as increasing the feeling of belonging, providing for quick feedback when ideas are suggested, focusing more clearly on primary purposes, and, in general, opening lines of positive communication between different levels of school leadership (Bagin and Gallagher, 2001).

Hanson (1991) identified eight methods of conflict management that include:

1. Expanding resources that are needed;
2. Having a clear appeals system so that parties can be heard;

3. Changing interaction patterns between conflicting individuals or groups;
4. Modifying the reward system when an actual or perceived inequity exists;
5. Merging the conflicting groups when conflict is moderate, and breaking up the group if the conflict is extreme;
6. Clarifying roles when ambiguity exists;
7. Consulting with a third party;
8. Accepting total responsibility by the superintendent for whatever occurs in the system, or becoming a conflict "sponge."

Another strategy for avoiding conflict when implementing school reform is to follow appropriate change actions. An example of successful change that has been empirically supported is the Concerns-Based Adoption Model (CBAM), which emphasizes the individuals involved and the innovation as a primary concern. There are three Concern Stages that when expanded into seven dimensions include awareness, informational, personal, management, impact, consequence, and collaboration and refocusing (Hall and Hord, 1987; Vaughan, 2002).

Harris (2000) suggests that in order to create a climate within our schools that fosters successful change efforts, school leaders must consider five critical factors. These factors, which all revolve around the question, "What is best for best for students?" include the role of culture cultivating the question, the role of leadership communicating the question, the role of teachers committing to the question, the role of accountability clarifying the question, and the role of change strategies always considering the question.

CASE STUDY

Lack of Support for the Superintendent's Recommendation

Superintendent Dr. Arthur Finley watched the news report on the ten o'clock evening news, relating the debacle at the regular monthly meeting of the Warner Independent School District (ISD) Board of Trustees. The story described the 4-3 vote against Finley's recommendation to employ Dr. Carol Garrison in succinct, professional terms. A human side to the story was told by veteran board member Anna Capel, "No,

I'm not really surprised that the board didn't go along with the superintendent's recommendation to hire another assistant superintendent. He needs to remember that there are some dynamics that are going on in our school district now that are quite different from the dynamics that were going on when we hired him."

Indeed, the dynamics were very different at that moment. Finley knew that the 4-3 vote had not really been about Dr. Garrison's qualifications for the position; the vote was a negative response to his reorganization of the central office staff. The recent retirement of veteran administrator Joe Elliott, an outspoken critic of many of the superintendent's actions, had opened an assistant superintendent position. With experience at the State Education Agency, Dr. Garrison had excellent credentials for the position. She and Finley had worked together as principals in the Melrose ISD in the early 1990s. Finley thought she was just the right person to provide leadership as assistant superintendent for Curriculum and Instruction.

Finley realized better than anyone that the school board who chose him three years earlier was not the same board he was working with today. There were three board members who were new to the board, elected just this past spring. One of the three new board members, Bruce Spencer, was a former principal of Warner High School. Spencer had taken early retirement rather than comply with changes instituted under Finley's leadership. While it had not been openly stated in public, it was generally understood that Spencer ran for the board to try to slow down district-wide changes that Finley advocated, including several very controversial personnel actions.

In the discussion that preceded the vote against the superintendent's recommendation that evening to hire Garrison, Spencer urged the board to take change more slowly, "We don't need to throw out the baby with the bath water." Spencer had also reminded the board the previous month, "There's no way the teacher's organization will support the curriculum revision plan, we need to think twice about this project."

Looking Back

Three years earlier, Finley had been the one chosen to lead the Warner ISD into the new millennium. Serving almost fifteen thousand students, the district was one of several smaller suburban districts near a large city. Former superintendent Dr. Susanna Holbrook had fought a valiant battle with cancer before her retirement. When she retired after nine years as superintendent, the school board had voiced commitment to higher standards of student learning, new models, and strategies of change. When Finley talked about best practices for students, curriculum development and implementation, and effective decision making based on sound research-based principles, the entire board had been in agreement.

When the board approved a District Improvement Plan that included goals for higher student achievement and an extensive curriculum project, Finley had taken the school board seriously and believed they were ready to support the change necessary to achieve these goals. It was soon apparent that changes in top leadership positions on several campuses would be necessary if these goals were to be achieved. East Side High School was one of those campuses.

East Side High School

One of the most controversial reassignments had been that of Dr. Carla McMath. Dr. McMath was principal of East Side High School, but had been reassigned to the principalship of the district's alternative school. She had been described by her supporters as a tough, fair-minded administrator who backed her teachers and ran a good school. The basic curriculum at East Side High School had included few electives and honors courses for a school that size, but the school was well organized and student discipline was exemplary.

She had hired most of the East Side High School faculty and staff during her ten years as principal, and most were very loyal to her. However, Dr. McMath's critics had described her as opinionated and unwilling to accept direction from the superintendent or anyone who challenged her. "A good one to have on your side, a bad one to have against you," observed one district administrator. After Dr. McMath's reassignment to the principalship at Pine Valley Alternative School, the district discipline center, she immediately resigned. Indeed, several school board members had questioned the superintendent about her reassignment and subsequent resignation, stressing her popularity with her faculty and many community members.

A Dysfunctional Team of Eight

Recent school board meetings had been the scenes of open division among board members and several high-profile clashes between the superintendent and board members Anna Capel, Bruce Spencer, Billy Walsh, and Pamela Cook. "It's all about educating children and we have to come to an understanding," stressed Cook . "We can't continue to fight among ourselves." Spencer had been less charitable in his remarks, "You can add our trustees and the superintendent together and you a have a dysfunctional team of eight."

The other three board members, Jack Watson, Leonard Hester, and Warren Bartlett, were still aligned with Superintendent Finley. Board member Bartlett had been quoted in a recent newspaper article calling for unity between the board and the superintendent. "I think we need to accept change in a positive light and look at it as a stepping stone to better things," he said. "We must do whatever it takes to make sure our kids get the high quality education they deserve."

Finley was discouraged, but not beaten. He still believed in the vision adopted by the board when he had been employed to lead the district. He still believed that the changes he had implemented were positive and in the best interests of the students in the district. Obviously, he had misjudged the level of support from the school board and underestimated how difficult change would be. How could he regain their support and help them once again focus on the district's educational vision?

DISCUSSION TOPICS/QUESTIONS

1. Discuss the implications of a changing school board on the local community.
2. How do internal and external political systems affect the superintendent?
3. Explain how the superintendent's knowledge of principles of conflict management could influence policy development within this district.
4. What are the legal parameters for a superintendent to consider in reassigning personnel?

5. Identify procedures to follow in reevaluating the educational vision of the district.
6. Pretend that you are the superintendent. What is the first step that you would implement to begin bringing about these personnel changes? Support your action.
7. Prepare and recommend policies for this district to improve student learning that are in compliance with state and federal requirements.
8. In a role-play with class members, use conflict resolution or mediation techniques to improve relationships with school board members.
9. Discuss the "concern-based adoption model" of change (Hord, Rutherford, Huling-Austin, and Hall, 1987), and identify steps for the superintendent to follow when implementing this strategy to bring about change.

REFERENCES

Bagin, D., and Gallagher, D. (2001). *The school and community relations* (7th ed.). Boston: Allyn & Bacon.

Farkas, S., Johnson, J., Duffett, A., and Foleno, T. (2001). *Trying to stay ahead of the game: Superintendents and principals talk about school leadership.* New York: Public Agenda.

Hall, G. E., and Hord, S. M. (1987). *Change in schools facilitating the process.* New York: State University of New York Press.

Hanson, E. Mark. (1991). *Educational administration and organizational behavior.* Boston: Allyn & Bacon.

Harris, S. (2000). Creating a climate for school reform that will last: Five critical factors. *Catalyst for Change, 30*(1), 11–13.

Hord, S., Rutherford, W., Huling-Austin, L., and Hall, G. (1987). *Taking charge of change.* Alexandria, VA: Association for Supervision and Curriculum Development.

Murphy, J. (2001). The changing face of leadership preparation. *The School Administrator, 10*(8), 14–17.

Owen, J., and Ovando, M. (2000). *Superintendent's guide to creating community.* Lanham, MD: Scarecrow Press.

Sternberg, R. (2002). The new job: Tailored fit or misfit? *The School Administrator, 59*(5), 6–15.

Storey, V. (2001). Dean, judge, and bishop: Lessons from a conflict and implications for school leaders. *International Electronic Journal for Leadership in Learning,* 5(17). Available online: www.ucalgary.ca/~iejll/volume5/Storey.html [accessed November 25, 2002].

Vaughan,W. (2002). Professional development and the adoption and implementation of new innovations: Do teacher concerns matter? *International Electronic Journal for Leadership in Learning, 6*(5). Available online: www.ucalgary.ca/~iejll/volume6/vaughan.html [accessed November 25, 2002].

ADDITIONAL RESOURCES

Ackerman, R., and Maslin-Ostrowski, P. (2002). *The wounded leader.* San Francisco: Jossey-Bass.

Hargreaves, A. (1994). *Changing teachers, changing times: Teachers' work and culture in the postmodern culture.* New York: Columbia University Press.

Rahim, M. A. (2001). *Managing conflict in organizations* (3rd ed.). Westport, CT: Quorum Books.

Ruble, T., and Schneer, J. (1994). Gender differences in conflict-handling styles. In *Conflict and gender* (pp. 155–167). Eds. A. Taylor and J.B. Miller. Cresskill, NJ: Hampton Press.

Stitt, A. J. (1998). *Alternative dispute resolution for organizations: How to design a system for effective resolution.* Canada: John Wiley & Sons.

CHAPTER 5

Higher Test Scores at Any Price?

Texas Standard—Competency 005:

The superintendent knows how to facilitate the planning and implementation of strategic plans that enhance teaching and learning; ensure alignment among curriculum, curriculum resources, and assessment; and promote the use of varied assessments to measure student performance.

ISLLC Standard 2:

A school administrator is an educational leader who promotes the success of all students by advocating, nurturing, and sustaining a school culture and instructional program conducive to student learning and staff professional development.

NCATE Standard 2:

Candidates who complete the program are educational leaders who have the knowledge and ability to promote the success of all students by promoting a positive school culture, providing an effective instructional program, applying best practice to student learning, and designing comprehensive professional growth plans for staff.

ABSTRACT

Two district administrators have resigned because of allegations that student scores on the mandated state academic achievement exam have been manipulated. The administrators blame their actions on pressure from the superintendent for the district to achieve recognized status. How can the superintendent balance the need for an effective, achievable campus plan with the community expectation of high student achievement?

OBJECTIVES

Objective 1: The superintendent knows how to implement planning procedures to develop curricula that achieve optimal student learning.

Objective 2: The superintendent knows how to evaluate district curricula and provide direction for improving curricula based on sound, research-based practices.

Objective 3: The superintendent knows how to implement multiple sources of information regarding academic performance for students.

Objective 4: The superintendent knows how to facilitate effective curricular decision making based on an understanding of pedagogy, curriculum design, cognitive development, learning processes, and child and adolescent growth and development.

Objective 5: The superintendent knows how to implement core curriculum design and delivery systems to ensure instructional quality and continuity across the district.

LITERATURE REVIEW

The controversy over high-stakes testing continues to rage in the United States. Many school boards, superintendents, and advocacy groups in the state of New York, for example, have passed resolutions asking for flexibility in a "testing scheme that provides absolutely no alternatives" (Cala, 2001, p. 12). But even though many school leaders have gone public with their concerns that this type of testing can actually do harm to schools, polls indicate that public opinion still shows strong support for testing (Riede, 2001). In fact, forty-nine states have begun initiatives to raise academic standards (Public Agenda, 2000), forty-eight states have adopted some form of mandated state assessment that requires students to pass in order to be promoted to the next grade (Rabinowitz, 2001), and nineteen states have mandated assessments that must be passed for a student to graduate from high school (Olson, 2000). At the same time, the results of these mandated student evaluations are often being used as the basis for accountability-based rewards and sanctions.

However, mandated state assessments have not completely replaced local assessments. In fact, Rabinowitz (2001) recommended that local districts continue to assess students to develop more detailed data for tracking student growth and identifying instructional strengths and weaknesses. These local programs should link to state and local content standards, provide information valued at the local level, and support teaching and learning.

It is up to school leaders at the local level to determine when performance-based assessments can provide much needed flexibility to multiple-choice assessments. Another model for district accountability was espoused by Richard Rothstein, a research associate with the Economic Policy Institute in Washington, D.C. Rothstein recommended a "composite index of school performance" (Schroeder and Pryor, 2001, p. 22) that includes standard competencies in core academic areas; it also recommends evaluating teacher quality, parental involvement, school facilities, class size, and school safety issues to determine school accountability issues.

In an effort to discourage administrators and classroom teachers from teaching to the test, Popham (2001) suggested that districts encourage and support curriculum teaching, which targets instruction focused on "test-represented content rather than at test items" (p. 17). Tomlinson (2001) recommended seven key principles to guide curriculum planning and instruction in order to account for standards: 1) reflect on the purpose of curriculum; 2) plan curriculum that addresses all aspects of learning; 3) plan curriculum that helps students make sense of things; 4) organize curriculum so that contents are manageable for teachers and students; 5) design instruction so that learning is invitational; 6) design instruction for focused action; and 7) design instruction that encompasses learner variance. In the high-pressure environment of high-stakes testing, two additional principles for effective teaching and learning are necessary: create a learning atmosphere that is typified by safety, respect, and trust, and teach for success.

It is the superintendent who is responsible for ethical, legal, implementation of district goals; and, ultimately, it is the superintendent's responsibility to lead in the challenge to ensure that all students learn. It is this goal that should guide the district's improvement agenda and all of the objectives that follow. Strategies that lead to this happening include intervening early to meet individual student needs, supporting student attendance, controlling class size, providing quality instruction, expecting excellence, working to help students come to school in good health, providing consistency for high-mobility students, providing time for basic courses, obtaining community support, assessing in multiple ways, aligning curriculum, instruction, and assessments, holding all gatekeepers accountable, building relationships among administration and faculty, identifying goals, providing feedback, and supporting effective teamwork (Johnson and Taylor, 2001).

CASE STUDY

The Resignations

Grant Thompson, Wilson High School principal, and Jeanette Brewer, Dean of Instruction, both resigned amid allegations that student records were manipulated to improve the school's rating on the State Assessment of Academic Skills (SAAS) test. Both Thompson and Brewer resigned before the school district's investigation was completed. Superintendent Charles Ransansky knew that both administrators would have been fired had they not quit.

Test Scores at Any Price?

The Neese Independent School District (ISD) began investigating in March after receiving an anonymous letter with detailed allegations about a scheme to improve the school's chances for a high-rating status. Ratings would be based on the district's performance on the mandated SAAS, which students had taken earlier in the year. Superintendent Ransansky had appointed an investigative team, led by the school district's attorney, Brian Chavez, and the director of testing and evaluation, Warren Edmonds. The team interviewed twenty-six Neese ISD employees, including Thompson and Brewer, as well as five students.

The investigation revealed that Brewer did violate district policies and procedures, State Education Agency rules, and SAAS rules and procedures. Investigation team leader Chavez reported to the superintendent that Brewer kept some students who might not score well from taking the test. She also voided the test scores of other students, Chavez said. Among their findings, the investigators reported that Brewer reviewed the answer sheets of twenty-four students, improperly voided some, and directed her secretary to void others. She also improperly exempted thirty-eight other students who should have taken the test.

The report also revealed that Principal Thompson was negligent because he had not monitored Brewer's activities sufficiently. When the probe began, Thompson was reassigned to the Athletic Department, and Brewer was placed on administrative leave.

Just the previous night on the evening news, Arlene Jackson, spokesperson for the State Education Agency, speculated that "the two administrators felt so much intense pressure to produce high SAAS scores that they lost sight of the purpose of the test." However, she continued, "State law prohibits altering or tampering with SAAS documents, therefore, the investigative report is still under review." She added that "criminal charges could be filed if it is found that SAAS documents were tampered with."

How Can the Superintendent Help?

Superintendent Ransansky picked up the district Academic Indicator of Student Success (AISS) report from the previous year that lay on his desk. What could he have done that might have prevented these two administrators from giving in to these temptations regarding the test? After all, there was a tremendous amount of pressure from the school board and from the community to see that all students in the district performed at top achievement levels. Could better planning have resulted in instructional gains, thereby, lessening the pressure to succeed at any cost?

DISCUSSION TOPICS/QUESTIONS

1. Construct a District Plan from the data in table 5.1. In your district plan identify goals, objectives, time-line, staffing, and budget allocations.

District Name: Neese ISD

Table 5.1. STATE EDUCATION AGENCY
Academic Excellence Indicator System 2000–2001
District Performance Accountability Rating: Academically Acceptable

	State	Region C	District	African American	Hispanic	White	Native American	Asian/ Pac. Is.	Male	Female	Econ. Disadv.	Special Educ.
SAAS % Passing												
Grade 3 (English)												
Reading 2001	86.8%	86.5%	78.0%	68.2%	83.0%	86.7%	—	*	76.6%	79.5%	75.2%	55.7%
2000	87.9%	89.2%	86.6%	81.3%	88.0%	95.5%	*	*	87.2%	87.5%	84.2%	84.7%
Math 2001	83.1%	82.1%	74.7%	64.3%	79.6%	84.3%	—	*	75.6%	73.7%	71.9%	70.3%
2000	80.6%	80.6%	75.2%	66.6%	76.6%	91.7%	*	*	74.7%	75.6%	71.7%	71.6%
All Tests 2001	78.2%	77.3%	67.8%	56.3%	72.9%	80.1%	—	*	68.1%	67.7%	64.2%	55.8%
2000	77.1%	77.4%	72.3%	62.6%	74.7%	89.4%	*	*	71.3%	73.3%	68.4%	70.9%
SAAS % Passing												
Grade 3 (Spanish)												
Reading 2001	76.7%	80.0%	45.5%	—	45.5%	—	—	—	*	42.9%	45.5%	—
2000	75.7%	72.9%	58.3%	—	58.3%	—	—	—	63.2%	52.9%	57.1%	*
Math 2001	83.5%	71.8%	54.5%	—	54.5%	—	—	—	*	57.1%	54.5%	—
2000	75.1%	78.7%	78.4%	—	78.4%	—	—	—	78.9%	77.8%	80.6%	*
All Tests 2001	71.5%	67.9%	36.4%	—	36.4%	—	—	—	*	42.9%	36.4%	—
2000	66.3%	60.7%	48.6%	—	48.6%	—	—	—	52.6%	44.4%	50.0%	*
SAAS % Passing												
Grade 4 (English)												
Reading 2001	90.8%	91.2%	87.0%	81.8%	88.0%	95.7%	*	*	85.8%	88.0%	84.8%	74.1%
2000	89.9%	90.6%	82.5%	85.1%	90.1%	97.2%	—	*	88.3%	90.7%	87.6%	82.4%
Writing 2001	89.2%	88.9%	80.4%	87.5%	91.5%	95.1%	*	*	88.2%	92.2%	89.4%	80.4%
2000	90.3%	90.3%	81.4%	90.1%	90.4%	96.2%	—	*	89.5%	93.4%	89.7%	90.0%
Math 2001	91.3%	91.6%	88.2%	82.0%	90.6%	96.2%	*	*	87.4%	89.0%	86.7%	80.6%
2000	87.1%	88.0%	88.0%	83.7%	87.2%	98.4%	—	*	89.3%	86.8%	85.6%	86.3%
All Tests 2001	81.6%	81.2%	77.7%	68.4%	80.8%	90.7%	*	*	76.1%	79.0%	74.8%	68.9%
2000	87.1%	88.0%	80.0%	73.2%	79.6%	94.2%	—	*	78.3%	81.7%	76.1%	76.8%

SAAS % Passing

Grade 4 (Spanish)

Reading	2001	66.4%	40.0%	50.0%	—	50.0%	—	—	—	*	*	50.0%	—
	2000	58.4%	37.8%	42.9%	—	42.9%	—	—	—	42.9%	42.9%	42.9%	—
Writing	2001	76.0%	29.6%	33.3%	—	33.3%	—	—	—	80.0%	*	37.5%	—
	2000	73.8%	73.0%	81.0%	—	81.0%	—	—	—	71.4%	85.7%	81.0%	—
Math	2001	89.3%	66.7%	55.6%	—	55.6%	—	—	—	60.0%	*	56.0%	*
	2000	77.0%	67.6%	81.0%	—	81.0%	—	—	—	100.0%	71.4%	81.0%	*
All Tests	2001	59.5%	25.8%	33.3%	—	33.3%	—	—	—	37.5%	*	36.4%	*
	2000	52.2%	34.2%	36.4%	—	36.4%	—	—	—	28.6%	40.0%	36.4%	—

SAAS % Passing

Grade 5 (English)

Reading	2001	90.2%	90.7%	90.4%	87.5%	89.9%	97.1%	—	100.0%	89.8%	91.0%	88.5%	87.9%
	2000	87.8%	90.3%	89.7%	85.8%	88.9%	97.8%	*	100.0%	87.9%	91.5%	87.7%	88.9%
Math	2001	94.6%	95.2%	86.9%	95.5%	97.4%	98.8%	—	100.0%	96.5%	97.4%	96.5%	97.2%
	2000	92.1%	93.7%	85.8%	94.5%	95.4%	98.4%	*	100.0%	95.8%	95.7%	94.8%	94.2%
All Tests	2001	88.2%	88.6%	88.9%	85.7%	88.6%	95.9%	—	100.0%	88.0%	89.8%	87.0%	90.0%
	2000	85.0%	87.4%	88.0%	84.0%	87.0%	96.3%	*	100.0%	87.0%	88.9%	85.7%	87.9%

SAAS % Passing

Grade 5 (Spanish)

Reading	2001	71.8%	60.0%	40.0%	—	40.0%	—	—	—	*	*	40.0%	—
	2000	52.6%	78.6%	*	—	*	—	—	—	*	*	*	—
Math	2001	87.1%	61.1%	*	—	*	—	—	—	*	*	*	—
	2000	76.8%	92.3%	*	—	*	—	—	—	*	*	*	—
All Tests	2001	69.6%	52.6%	40.0%	—	40.0%	—	—	—	*	*	40.0%	—
	2000	50.3%	78.6%	*	—	*	—	—	—	*	*	*	—

SAAS % Passing

Grade 6 (English)

Reading	2001	85.6%	86.3%	82.5%	79.9%	79.2%	93.9%	—	100.0%	78.8%	85.9%	79.7%	72.1%
	2000	86.0%	87.1%	82.6%	80.3%	79.7%	93.7%	*	*	79.3%	85.7%	80.6%	65.7%

(continued)

Table 5.1. State Education Agency (continued)

		State	Region C	District	African American	Hispanic	White	Native American	Asian/ Pac. Is.	Male	Female	Econ. Disadv.	Special Educ.
Math	2001	91.4%	92.4%	81.7%	90.9%	89.8%	97.0%	*	100.0%	88.7%	94.7%	90.7%	85.1%
	2000	88.5%	89.7%	87.9%	84.8%	87.4%	96.0%	*	*	86.2%	89.5%	86.3%	75.0%
All Tests	2001	82.7%	83.4%	80.0%	76.3%	76.8%	93.5%	*	100.0%	75.9%	84.0%	76.9%	69.8%
	2000	81.5%	82.7%	77.6%	73.2%	75.6%	91.6%	*	*	74.6%	80.5%	75.0%	64.9%
SAAS % Passing Grade 7													
Reading	2001	89.4%	91.4%	89.9%	86.1%	90.4%	96.5%	*	*	88.5%	91.0%	88.2%	69.7%
	2000	83.5%	85.2%	76.4%	74.0%	72.2%	91.4%	*	*	76.4%	76.3%	71.4%	53.6%
Math	2001	89.6%	91.4%	71.9%	89.1%	93.2%	94.6%	*	*	91.8%	92.0%	91.0%	72.2%
	2000	88.1%	89.8%	88.6%	83.7%	90.8%	94.8%	*		89.0%	88.1%	85.9%	75.9%
All Tests	2001	84.3%	86.4%	85.1%	79.8%	87.2%	91.3%			84.4%	85.7%	82.9%	68.4%
	2000	79.3%	81.2%	71.3%	66.6%	69.0%	87.9%			71.2%	71.5%	65.5%	50.0%
SAAS % Passing Grade 8													
Reading	2001	91.9%	93.8%	91.1%	89.9%	89.3%	97.7%	*	*	90.5%	91.8%	88.7%	72.2%
	2000	89.6%	91.4%	91.5%	87.7%	92.7%	95.5%	*	*	90.4%	92.3%	90.1%	85.2%
Writing	2001	85.8%	85.5%	81.2%	79.2%	77.5%	94.0%	*	*	75.2%	87.3%	76.5%	64.7%
	2000	84.3%	84.2%	74.8%	69.9%	69.1%	92.7%	*	*	66.9%	80.9%	69.6%	44.4%
Math	2001	92.4%	93.5%	92.5%	89.3%	93.1%	98.5%	*	*	92.6%	92.3%	91.2%	90.9%
	2000	90.2%	92.3%	93.1%	90.7%	93.0%	97.2%	*	*	93.1%	93.2%	91.7%	86.2%
Science	2001	91.8%	93.3%	84.0%	78.8%	83.9%	96.2%	*	*	83.6%	84.8%	80.9%	55.0%
	2000	88.2%	89.6%	82.7%	76.6%	81.5%	94.9%	*	*	82.0%	83.3%	80.5%	76.7%
Social S.	2001	77.0%	77.4%	64.8%	58.1%	64.0%	81.2%	*	*	66.1%	83.4%	60.1%	57.9%
	2000	71.8%	73.2%	57.6%	52.5%	52.7%	75.0%	*	*	62.0%	54.3%	52.2%	40.0%
All Tests	2000	69.2%	68.4%	56.7%	50.3%	53.8%	77.7%	*	*	55.7%	57.8%	50.2%	58.6%
	2001	64.6%	65.0%	47.9%	40.8%	41.8%	71.2%	*	*	47.8%	47.9%	40.3%	31.6%

SAAS % Passing
Grade 10

Reading	2001	90.0%	90.3%	82.3%	75.7%	80.6%	95.7%	*	80.0%	80.0%	84.1%	80.1%	52.3%
	2000	90.3%	90.6%	81.2%	79.9%	76.4%	94.4%	*	*	76.6%	85.7%	78.3%	60.5%
Writing	2001	89.1%	88.1%	77.4%	76.7%	73.9%	85.3%	*	80.0%	72.4%	81.6%	75.6%	45.7%
	2000	90.7%	91.3%	81.0%	81.3%	75.5%	92.2%	*	*	76.8%	85.0%	76.7%	50.0%
Math	2001	89.3%	89.8%	85.4%	78.9%	87.0%	93.2%	*	100.0%	85.3%	85.5%	84.6%	62.1%
	2000	86.8%	87.3%	77.5%	71.7%	77.3%	88.8%	*	*	74.9%	80.1%	74.4%	55.6%
All Tests	2001	80.3%	79.5%	44.3%	56.7%	62.5%	80.1%	*	80.0%	59.2%	68.7%	61.9%	29.8%
	2000	80.4%	81.8%	55.9%	61.4%	61.3%	83.7%	*	*	59.3%	72.4%	60.5%	33.3%

**Credit for End-of–Course examinations is not included in the passing rate.

Percent of Failers Passing SAAS

Reading	2001	52.2%	55.4%	54.2%	52.4%	53.4%	75.8%	—	—	55.3%	52.9%	52.6%	50.0%
	2000	49.0%	51.4%	51.8%	46.5%	55.1%	65.5%	—	*	46.4%	57.5%	50.1%	41.0%
Math	2001	57.4%	61.4%	56.2%	60.8%	71.2%	90.0%	*	—	67.2%	65.4%	66.8%	57.1%
	2000	49.8%	52.9%	59.1%	56.8%	59.7%	76.5%	*	—	60.5%	57.7%	59.3%	70.6%

SAAS % Passing (Sum of 3–8 and 10)
Accountability Subset ***

Reading	2001	88.9%	90.0%	85.5%	81.1%	85.5%	94.6%	100.0%	95.8%	84.0%	87.0%	83.2%	67.2%
	2000	87.4%	89.1%	85.2%	82.0%	83.4%	95.3%	100.0%	90.9%	83.5%	86.8%	82.9%	75.9%
Writing	2001	87.9%	87.5%	83.5%	82.0%	81.6%	91.3%	80.0%	72.7%	79.3%	87.4%	81.9%	66.0%
	2000	88.2%	88.5%	83.0%	81.1%	79.3%	93.8%	80.0%	80.0%	79.0%	86.7%	80.0%	61.5%
Math	2001	90.2%	90.8%	88.3%	83.9%	89.5%	94.4%	87.5%	100.0%	87.7%	88.9%	86.9%	78.5%
	2000	87.4%	88.8%	86.4%	81.8%	86.7%	95.3%	92.3%	90.9%	86.1%	86.7%	84.4%	78.0%
All Tests	2001	82.1%	82.5%	77.0%	70.7%	77.5%	88.8%	87.5%	88.0%	74.9%	79.1%	74.2%	63.6%
	2000	79.9%	81.2%	75.3%	69.6%	73.3%	90.7%	84.6%	86.4%	72.8%	77.7%	71.6%	64.5%

***The Accountability Subset for this district includes 0 students in 2001, and 2 students in 2000 who qualified for End-of–Course exam credit and did not take the exit-level Texas Assessment of Academic Skills (TAAS) test.

(continued)

Table 5.1. State Education Agency (continued)

	State	Region C	District	African American	Hispanic	White	Native American	Asian/ Pac. Is.	Male	Female	Econ. Disadv.	Special Educ.
SAAS Cumulative Pass Rate—Exit												
Class of 2001	93.1%	92.2%	80.9%	77.7%	77.7%	93.1%	—	66.7%	80.4%	81.3%	n/a	n/a
Class of 2000	91.6%	91.4%	83.3%	84.8%	73.0%	92.7%	*	100.0%	84.0%	82.5%	n/a	n/a
End-of-Course Exam (% Passing)												
(Preview of 2003 Exit Level)												
Algebra I												
% Passing												
2001	49.2%	46.6%	30.2%	27.2%	27.2%	43.4%	*	*	30.1%	30.3%	27.1%	6.8%
2000	43.9%	42.0%	30.5%	11.8%	22.4%	32.8%	*	25.0%	20.1%	21.1%	18.6%	6.9%
Biology												
% Passing												
2001	79.9%	83.7%	45.0%	55.3%	61.4%	89.9%	*	100.0%	68.3%	62.0%	61.5%	30.8%
2000	80.3%	82.2%	61.5%	51.2%	61.7%	82.4%	*	100.0%	64.4%	58.9%	57.2%	30.0%
English II												
% Passing												
2001	75.1%	75.5%	56.3%	47.3%	54.8%	74.1%	*	57.1%	47.3%	64.1%	52.2%	34.6%
2000	77.7%	75.9%	56.0%	46.5%	60.2%	67.6%	*	*	42.0%	69.1%	54.4%	41.2%
U.S. History												
% Passing												
2001	74.3%	73.8%	62.1%	55.3%	60.4%	79.1%	*	*	63.7%	60.6%	56.7%	34.0%
2000	72.1%	72.2%	46.9%	39.1%	40.0%	68.8%	—	*	57.0%	36.5%	48.2%	17.6%
End-of-Course Exam (% Taking)												
Attendance Rate												
1999–2000	95.6%	96.0%	94.9%	95.0%	94.7%	95.1%	94.3%	97.6%	95.0%	94.8%	95.6%	94.1%
1998–1999	95.4%	95.8%	94.6%	94.3%	94.7%	95.0%	93.8%	97.2%	94.6%	94.6%	94.9%	93.5%
Annual Dropout Rate (Gr. 7–12)												
1999–2000	1.3%	1.1%	2.8%	3.3%	2.9%	1.8%	0.0%	3.3%	3.4%	2.2%	1.7%	2.4%
1998–1999	1.6%	1.3%	3.1%	3.3%	3.5%	2.2%	7.1%	3.0%	3.3%	2.8%	2.4%	3.1%
Completion Rate/Student Status Rate												
Class of 2000												
% Graduated	80.7%	83.5%	64.2%	62.1%	62.3%	69.3%	—	*	61.3%	67.1%	54.7%	45.5%
% Received GED	4.8%	5.5%	8.4%	5.1%	7.4%	14.6%	—	*	7.6%	9.1%	9.1%	4.0%

	1	2	3	4	5	6	7	8	9	10	11	12
% Continued HS	7.3%	4.9%	24.2%	16.6%	17.6%	6.8%	—	*	15.5%	13.0%	17.1%	33.7%
% Dropped Out (4yr)	7.2%	6.1%	13.2%	16.2%	12.7%	9.3%	—	*	15.5%	10.9%	19.1%	16.8%
Class of 1999												
% Graduated	79.5%	82.4%	67.7%	64.0%	65.8%	75.7%	*	85.7%	62.6%	72.3%	70.0%	45.8%
% Received GED	4.0%	4.8%	6.9%	6.4%	6.4%	8.9%	*	0.0%	8.0%	5.9%	7.0%	1.2%
% Continued HS	8.0%	5.8%	13.4%	15.5%	13.7%	10.1%	*	0.0%	15.4%	11.6%	8.7%	37.3%
% Dropped Out(4yr)	8.5%	6.9%	12.0%	14.1%	14.1%	5.3%	*	14.3%	13.9%	10.2%	14.3%	15.7%
% Adv. Courses												
1999–2000	20.1%	15.9%	6.2%	4.2%	4.1%	13.2%	0.0%	20.0%	4.8%	7.7%	2.9%	1.2%
1998–1999	20.1%	14.6%	6.0%	2.9%	4.3%	14.0%	0.0%	23.8%	5.0%	7.1%	3.4%	1.4%
% Rec. HS Pgm.												
Class of 2000	38.6%	34.7%	19.1%	8.6%	17.1%	37.1%	—	*	17.6%	20.7%	12.4%	5.4%
Class of 1999	15.0%	13.6%	2.3%	0.5%	0.0%	9.5%	*	0.0%	1.3%	3.8%	0.0%	0.0%
AP/IB Results												
% Tested												
2000–2001	14.3%	10.0%	15.1%	10.1%	11.5%	29.9%	*	25.0%	11.6%	18.2%	n/a	n/a
1999–2000	12.7%	8.2%	5.1%	0.6%	3.7%	14.2%	—	33.3%	3.3%	6.7%	n/a	n/a
SAAS/SASP Equiv.												
Class of 2000	58.5%	59.4%	40.3%	22.0%	34.9%	71.8%	—	*	44.2%	37.0%	27.9%	15.4%
Class of 1999	53.5%	54.7%	33.3%	23.5%	26.7%	57.0%	*	50.0%	34.8%	32.0%	20.9%	5.6%
SAT/ACT Results												
% At/Above Crit.												
Class of 2000	27.3%	24.8%	24.1%	1.2%	2.9%	31.3%	—	*	11.7%	16.2%	n/a	n/a
Class of 1999	27.2%	23.9%	17.3%	4.8%	3.8%	33.3%	*	20.0%	16.5%	18.0%	n/a	n/a
% Tested												
Class of 2000	62.2%	58.4%	41.3%	40.3%	24.1%	59.7%	—	*	42.9%	39.9%	n/a	n/a
Class of 1999	61.8%	60.4%	36.1%	35.2%	18.2%	63.7%	*	62.5%	40.7%	36.0%	n/a	n/a
Mean SAT I Score												
Class of 2000	990	984	897	759	847	1025	—	*	897	897	n/a	n/a
Class of 1999	989	979	235	804	933	1033	—	*	949	927	n/a	n/a

(continued)

Table 5.1. State Education Agency (continued)

	State	Region C	District	African American	Hispanic	White	Native American	Asian/ Pac. Is.	Male	Female	Econ. Disadv.	Special Educ.
Mean ACT Score												
Class of 2000	20.3	20.4	17.3	15.1	17.8	20.1	*	—	16.3	18.1	n/a	n/a
Class of 1999	20.2	20.3	18.1	17.1	16.8	20.7	*	*	16.6	19.6	n/a	n/a

District Name: Neese ISD

State Education Agency
Academic Excellence Indicator System 2000–2001
District Profile: Neese ISD

Section II

STUDENT INFORMATION

		District		State	
		Count	Percent	Count	Percent
Total Students:		15,433	100.0%	4,059,619	100.0%
Students by Grade:	Early Childhood Education	49	0.3%	13,707	0.3%
	Pre-Kindergarten	681	4.4%	132,064	3.3%
	Kindergarten	1,293	8.4%	294,127	7.2%
	Grade 1	1,397	9.1%	320,752	7.9%
	Grade 2	1,240	8.0%	316,896	7.8%
	Grade 3	1,259	8.2%	316,535	7.8%
	Grade 4	1,244	8.1%	313,731	7.7%
	Grade 5	1,176	7.6%	311,638	7.7%
	Grade 6	1,150	7.5%	308,392	7.6%
	Grade 7	1,220	7.9%	310,696	7.7%
	Grade 8	1,052	6.8%	304,419	7.5%
	Grade 9	1,291	8.4%	360,704	8.9%
	Grade 10	1,056	6.8%	287,355	7.1%
	Grade 11	664	4.3%	248,570	6.1%
	Grade 12	661	4.3%	219,943	5.4%

Ethnic Distribution:	District		State	
African American	5,963	38.6%	585,609	14.4%
Hispanic	6,346	41.1%	1,646,508	40.6%
White	3,041	19.7%	1,706,989	42.0%
Asian/Pacific Islander	66	0.4%	108,422	2.7%
Native American	17	0.1%	12,091	0.3%
Economically Disadvantaged	11,660	75.6%	2,001,697	49.3%
Limited English Proficient (LEP)	1,613	10.5%	570,453	14.1%
Students with Disciplinary Placements (1999–2000)	591	4.0%	86,071	2.3%
Data Quality: PID Errors (Student)	49	30.0%	68,368	1.5%
Underreported Students	7	0.1%	19,718	1.0%

Retention Rates by Grade:	Nonspecial Education Rates		Special Education Rates	
	District	State	District	State
Kindergarten	2.5%	2.3%	11.8%	8.6%
Grade 1	8.4%	5.8%	8.7%	10.4%
Grade 2	4.9%	3.1%	1.9%	4.4%
Grade 3	6.4%	2.2%	1.7%	2.7%
Grade 4	2.5%	1.3%	1.9%	1.7%
Grade 5	3.1%	0.8%	2.0%	2.0%
Grade 6	7.3%	1.6%	4.0%	2.1%
Grade 7	10.7%	2.8%	6.8%	3.3%
Grade 8	6.5%	1.9%	2.7%	3.4%

	Counts	
	District	State
Graduates (Class of 2000):		
Total (Includes Special Education)	538	212,925
African American	221	27,507
Hispanic	164	68,314
White	151	109,721
Asian/Pacific Islander	2	6,862
Native American	0	521

(continued)

Table 5.1. State Education Agency *(continued)*

	Count	Percent
Special Education Graduates	56	19,982
Graduated Under Advanced Programs	0	2,635
Graduated Under Rec. HS Pgm./DAP	103	82,186

STAFF INFORMATION

		District		State	
		Count	Percent	Count	Percent
Professional Staff:					
	Teachers	1,255.2	61.5%	335,316.7	61.9%
		1,038.3	50.9%	274,816.7	50.8%
	Professional Support	149.0	7.3%	42,092.2	7.8%
	Campus Administration (School Leadership)	60.8	3.0%	13,916.5	2.6%
	Central Administration	7.0	0.3%	4,491.3	0.8%
Educational Aides:		102.9	5.0%	55,466.8	10.2%
Auxiliary Staff:		683.2	33.5%	150,599.4	27.8%
Total Staff:		2,041.4	100.0%	541,342.9	100.0%
Total Minority Staff:		877.5	43.0%	206,754.5	38.2%
Teachers by Ethnicity and Sex:					
	Females	831.4	80.1%	212,421.9	77.3%
	Males	207.0	19.9%	62,394.8	22.7%
	African American	214.2	20.6%	24,277.7	8.8%
	Hispanic	60.3	5.8%	46,969.6	17.1%
	White	750.9	72.3%	201,144.6	73.2%
	Asian/Pacific Islander	9.0	0.9%	1,725.0	0.6%
	Native American	4.0	0.4%	699.8	0.3%
Teachers by Highest Degree Held:					
	No Degree	6.0	0.6%	3,679.4	1.3%
	Bachelors	823.9	79.4%	205,423.8	74.7%
	Masters	202.3	19.5%	64,400.0	23.4%
	Doctorate	6.1	0.6%	1,287.8	0.5%

Teachers by Years of Experience:

	District	District	State	State
Beginning Teachers	112.4	10.8%	21,493.2	7.8%
1–5 Years' Experience	227.8	21.9%	75,174.0	27.4%
6–10 Years' Experience	171.2	16.5%	49,717.2	18.1%
11–20 Years' Experience	269.5	26.0%	69,508.6	25.3%
Over 20 Years' Experience	257.4	24.8%	58,923.6	21.4%
Number of Students per Teacher:	14.9	n/a	14.8	n/a

	District	State
Average Years Experience of Teachers:	13.2 yrs.	11.9 yrs.
Average Years Experience of Teachers with District:	9.1 yrs.	7.9 yrs.

Average Teacher Salary by Years of Experience: (regular duties only):

	District	State
Beginning Teachers	$23,253	$29,824
1–5 Years' Experinece	$27,258	$31,987
6–10 Years' Experience	$33,016	$35,304
11–20 Years' Experience	$39,589	$41,755
Over 20 Years' Experience	$44,598	$48,183

Average Actual Salaries (regular duties only):

	District	State
Teachers	$35,274	$38,361
Professional Support	$43,096	$45,462
Campus Administration (School Leadership)	$54,562	$58,081
Central Administration	$75,097	$69,916

Permits by Type:

	District	State
Emergency (for certified personnel)	9	3,519
Emergency (for uncertified personnel)	27	7,418
Nonrenewable	18	2,253
Temporary Classroom Assignment	4	927
District Teaching	6	461
Temporary Exemption	0	31
Turnover Rate for Teachers:	20.8%	16.0%

(continued)

Table 5.1. State Education Agency (*continued*)

TAX INFORMATION

	District		State	
	Amount	Percent/Rate	Amount	Percent/Rate
Adopted Tax Rate (calendar year 2000)				
Maintenance and Operations	n/a	$1.441	n/a	$1.384
Interest and Sinking Fund	n/a	$0.140	n/a	$0.091
Total Rate (sum of above)	n/a	$1.581	n/a	$1.475
Standardized Local Tax Base (comptroller valuation)				
Value (after exemptions)	$2,153,456,626	n/a	$864,265,433,673	n/a
Value per Pupil	$139,536	n/a	$215,232	n/a
Value by Category				
Business	$1,263,306,617	49.1%	$384,002,276,669	39.0%
Residential	$1,235,497,271	48.0%	$493,051,546,220	50.1%
Land	$44,697,903	1.7%	$68,963,816,777	7.0%
Oil and Gas	$0	0.0%	$28,283,870,983	2.9%
Other	$29,133,677	1.1%	$10,351,770,594	1.1%
BUDGETED REVENUE INFORMATION				
Total Revenues	$98,461,056	n/a	$26,115,722,356	n/a
Total Revenues per Pupil	$6,380	n/a	$6,433	n/a
Revenues by Source				
Local Tax	$35,135,775	35.7%	$12,663,733,663	48.5%
Other Local & Intermediate	$3,495,990	3.6%	$1,190,208,713	4.6%
State	$54,087,992	54.9%	$11,377,498,894	43.6%
Federal	$5,741,299	5.8%	$884,281,086	3.4%

BUDGETED EXPENDITURE INFORMATION

	District		State	
	Amount	Percent	Amount	Percent
Total Expenditures:	$99,631,102	100.0%	$26,948,681,700	100.0%
Total Expenditures by Object:				
Operating	$90,014,645	90.3%	$24,970,204,499	89.4%
Payroll Costs (6100)	$69,813,517	70.1%	$19,810,622,664	73.5%
Professional & Contracted Services (6200)	$11,404,845	11.4%	$2,125,058,228	7.9%
	$11,404,845	7.2%	$1,692,789,691	6.3%
	$7,177,037	1.6%	$468,733,916	1.7%
Debt Service (6500)	$9,616,457	9.7%	$2,851,477,201	10.6%
Capital Outlay (6600)	$6,521,418	6.5%	$2,230,081,138	8.3%
	$3,095,039	3.1%	$621,396,063	2.3%
Total Operating Expenditures by Function:	$88,891,181	100.0%	$24,010,804,383	100.0%
Instruction (11, 95)	$48,058,835	54.1%	$13,880,333,499	57.8%
Instruction–Related Services (12, 13)	$1,675,557	1.9%	$711,993,126	3.0%
Instructional Leadership (21)	$1,879,270	2.1%	$327,217,968	1.4%
School Leadership (23)	$6,569,009	7.4%	$1,413,048,962	5.9%
Support Services–Student (31, 32, 33)	$3,985,151	4.5%	$1,080,558,025	4.5%
Student Transportation (34)	$2,483,945	2.8%	$676,770,906	2.8%
Food Service (35)	$6,548,725	7.4%	$1,315,831,789	5.5%
Cocurricular/Extracurricular Activities (36)	$2,438,831	2.7%	$601,620,200	2.5%
Central Administration (41, 92)	$3,031,884	3.4%	$953,749,911	4.0%
Plant Maintenance and Operations (51)	$10,188,792	11.5%	$2,598,036,618	10.8%
Security and Monitoring Services (52)	$847,688	1.0%	$153,117,054	0.6%
Data Processing Services (53)	$1,183,494	1.3%	$298,526,325	1.2%

(continued)

Table 5.1. State Education Agency *(continued)*

BUDGETED EXPENDITURE INFORMATION (continued)

Per Pupil Expenditures:

	District	State
Total Expenditures	$6,456	$6,638
Total Operating Expenditures by Function	$5,760	$5,915
Instruction (11, 95) & Instruct. Leadership (21)	$3,236	$3,500
School Leadership (23)	$426	$348
Central Administration (41,92)	$196	$235
Other Operating (12, 13, 31–36, 51–53)	$1,902	$1,832
Total Expenditures for Community Services	$1,090,697	$68,769,233
Total Expenditures for Athletic Programs	$2,534,114	$433,991,361

PROGRAM INFORMATION

	District		State	
	Count	Percent	Count	Percent
Student Enrollment by Programs:				
Bilingual/ESL Education	1,332	8.6%	509,885	12.6%
Career and Technology Education	3,071	19.9%	768,200	18.9%
Gifted and Talented Education	1,359	8.8%	342,840	8.4%
Special Education	2,486	16.1%	483,442	11.9%
Teachers by Program (population served):				
Bilingual/ESL Education	28.1	2.7%	20,515.7	7.5%
Career and Technology Education	42.5	4.1%	11,810.7	4.3%
Compensatory Education	8.4	0.8%	8,947.2	3.3%
Gifted and Talented Education	47.8	4.6%	6,099.3	2.2%
Regular Education	775.7	74.7%	193,474.5	70.4%
Special Education	124.0	11.9%	27,298.5	9.9%
Other	11.9	1.1%	6,670.8	2.4%

Budgeted Instructional Operating Expenditures by Program:	Amount	Percent	Amount	Percent
Bilingual/ESL Education	$1,951,990	4.1%	$590,748,041	4.3%
Career and Technology Education	$1,882,413	3.9%	$566,681,113	4.1%
Compensatory Education	$3,263,057	6.8%	$911,525,819	6.6%
Gifted and Talented Education	$496,188	1.0%	$245,961,232	1.8%
Regular Education	$34,473,941	71.7%	$9,798,493,253	70.7%
Special Education	$5,991,246	12.5%	$1,739,689,310	12.6%

CLASS SIZE INFORMATION

(Derived from teacher responsibility records.)

Class Size Averages by Grade and Subject:

Elementary:	District	State
Kindergarten	19.0	18.8
Grade 1	18.8	18.1
Grade 2	18.2	18.7
Grade 3	19.8	19.0
Grade 4	19.2	19.8
Grade 5	21.7	22.6
Grade 6	21.9	22.5
Mixed Grades	28.2	23.2
Secondary:		
English/Language Arts	20.4	20.2
Foreign Languages	21.3	20.9
Mathematics	20.3	20.3
Science	21.8	21.6
Social Studies	23.8	22.7

2. Identify professional development needs for staff based on the district plan that you have designed.

3. Identify special programs needed for your district.

4. What strategies will you implement to facilitate the cooperation of the faculty, the school board, and the larger school community in achieving this district plan?

5. In what ways are strategic planning and constructing a district plan based on the data alike? How might they be different?

REFERENCES

Cala, W. (2001). My fight for an alternative diploma. *The School Administrator, 58*(11), 2–14.

Johnson, C., and Taylor, R. (2001). Excellence for all in Minneapolis. *Educational Leadership, 58*(6), 5–59.

Olson, L. (2000, April 5). Worries of a standards "backlash" grow. *Education Week,* 1, 12–13.

Popham, W. J. (2001). Teaching to the test? *Educational Leadership, 58*(6), 16–20.

Public Agenda. (2000, February 16). Reality check 2000. *Education Week,* SI–S8.

Rabinowitz, S. (2001). Balancing state and local assessments. *The School Administrator, 11*(58), 16–21.

Riede, P. (2001). Testing dissidents. *The School Administrator, 11*(58), 6–11.

Schroeder, F., and Pryor, S. (2001). Multiple measures: Beginning with ends. *The School Administrator, 11*(58), 22–25.

Tomlinson, C. (2001). Grading for success. *Educational Leadership, 58*(6), 12–15.

ADDITIONAL RESOURCES

Creighton, T. (2001). *Schools and data: The educator's guide for improved decision-making.* Thousand Oaks, CA: Corwin Press.

Dooley, D. (2001). *Social research methods* (4th ed.). Upper Saddle River, NJ: Prentice Hall.

Lissitz, R., and Schafer, W. (2002). *Assessment in educational reform.* Boston: Allyn & Bacon.

CHAPTER 6

Se Habla Español Aqui?

Texas Standard—Competency 006:
The superintendent knows how to advocate, nurture, and sustain an instructional program and a district culture that are conducive to student learning and staff professional growth.

ISLLC Standard 2:
A school administrator is an educational leader who promotes the success of all students by advocating, nurturing, and sustaining a school culture and instructional program conducive to student learning and staff professional growth.

NCATE 2:
Candidates who complete the program are educational leaders who have the knowledge and ability to promote the success of all students by promoting a positive school culture, providing an effective instructional program, applying best practice to student learning, and designing comprehensive professional growth plans for staff.

ABSTRACT

The superintendent is responsible for advocating, nurturing, and sustaining an instructional program that benefits all students within the district. As the job of the superintendent shifts from management, it has become more concerned with teaching and learning. This case presents the dilemma that faces a superintendent when achievement declines as the community experiences diverse population changes.

OBJECTIVES

Objective 1: The superintendent must facilitate the development of a learning organization that encourages educational excellence, supports instructional improvement, and incorporates best practice.

Objective 2: The superintendent applies knowledge of special programs to ensure that students with special needs are provided with appropriate resources and effective, flexible instructional programs and services.

Objective 3: The superintendent knows how to analyze instructional resource needs and deploy instructional resources effectively and equitably for student learning.

Objective 4: The superintendent ensures responsiveness to diverse sociological, linguistic, cultural, psychological, and other factors that may affect student development and learning and create an environment in which all students can learn.

LITERATURE REVIEW

In the most successful schools in the United States, the level of support from administration includes frequent supervision for the purpose of improving learning for all students (Glickman, 2002). Leadership in these effective schools understands that the "direct improvement of teaching and learning in every classroom" (p. 2) only happens when leaders emphasize continual reflection and changing of classroom practices guided by best practice (Glickman, 2002). Student learning must be the central focus of all that happens in the school setting.

It is the role of the superintendent to guide staff in implementing elements that influence student learning in schools. According to Glickman (2002) these elements include:

1. Elements that directly influence student learning, such as content, methods, and assessment;
2. Elements that organize instructional leaders' work with teachers, such as focus for observations and how to use data, approaches to work with teachers, and structures and formats for organizing improvement efforts; and

3. Elements that provide the overarching context for instructional improvement, such as school renewal priorities, professional development, and evaluation. (p.7)

However, before instructional excellence can be achieved for students, superintendents must lead school communities to a better understanding of diverse, cultural influences. The cultural environment of today's schools is rapidly changing due to the diverse population within the United States. For example, nearly 40 percent of public school classrooms consisted of children of color in 1993 (Kuhlman and Vidal, 1993), and census data predict that by 2050 this number will be nearly 50 percent (U.S. Bureau of the Census, 1998).

Multiculturalism, while it helps groups understand their own cultural heritage, also contributes to understanding and building respect for other cultures (Simmons, 1998). Therefore, the superintendent must lead the charge to recruit and hire faculty members from minority groups to serve as role models, must provide staff development with a multicultural pedagogy for all faculty, and must exhibit cultural sensitivity and responsiveness to staff, students, and the community in all decisions (Echols and Stader, 2002).

Unfortunately, there is a continuing debate over the best way to educate children from linguistically and culturally different backgrounds. In fact, some educators support eliminating bilingual programs, while other critics have challenged the very heart of multicultural education and related reforms that accommodate cultural as well as linguistic diversity. However, a national survey sponsored by the National Center for Education Statistics recently reported that while 54 percent of the teachers had Limited English Proficient (LEP) students in classrooms, only 20 percent felt prepared to teach them (Mora, 2000).

At the same time, legal mandates support multicultural teaching and require schools to provide effective programs for schooling children from diverse student populations. Thus, it is imperative that the superintendent support a risk-free environment for curriculum to address the many issues affecting culturally diverse children in mainstream classrooms.

Superintendents also must support the identifying of factors that will better motivate parental involvement of LEP students. Some of these factors include supporting faculty in conducting home visits, offering flexible times for parental conferences, providing transportation for parents, and celebrating the community's diverse cultures and traditions (Cassity and Harris, 2000).

The culture of the school permeates every aspect of the school day because it is all that goes on within the school: the norms, attitudes, beliefs, and behaviors. Barth (2002) identifies "the most important and the most difficult job of an instructional leader" as that of changing the culture of a school (p. 6). This challenge to change a school culture requires that the leader be able to lead the school community in replacing unhealthy elements with desirable qualities, such as building trust, having high expectations, communicating with the learning community, and encouraging an environment for experimentation (Barth, 2002).

In order for school leaders to support school improvement they must recognize that the role of instructional leadership may vary in communities depending on school needs. By keeping the focus on "improving teaching and learning and on gathering evidence of student achievement that demonstrates this improvement" (King, 2002, p. 62). This includes leading learning by participating in collaborative, professional learning experiences; focusing on teaching and learning by helping teachers improve and by placing the highest priority on student achievement; developing leadership capacity by involving every level of the school community in the important work of educating children; creating conditions for professional learning by fostering collaboration and personal growth; using data to inform decisions; and using resources creatively by encouraging the use of people, time, and money for supporting improvement within the school (King, 2002).

CASE STUDY

Superintendent John Fletcher was concerned, very concerned. The population of his school district was growing dramatically and diversely — but that was not a problem. The growth was creating a situation that he was not sure how to address.

Background

Over the past few years, declining mineral values had dealt a strong financial blow to the McKay Independent School District (ISD). As the property wealth of the district declined, the superintendent at the time, James Elders, had been forced to cut programs. The General Educational Development (GED) Program had been eliminated, along with several other programs and initiatives. Counselors had been reassigned to teaching positions at each elementary school, and the district's community outreach program had significant budget cuts. When Elders resigned, Fletcher was hired to replace him.

Fletcher, now in his third year as superintendent of the McKay ISD, had just received confirmation that the Fresh Farms Poultry Processing Plant would be expanding their workforce. This was good news for the community. The expansion would create jobs for five hundred people and would hopefully bring another new surge of economic life to the area. This expansion would also cause a significant increase in the number of low-wage, labor-intensive jobs. Most of the individuals taking these jobs would be Spanish speaking with little or no schooling in the United States and speaking and reading little or no English. Their children would enter the McKay ISD soon.

Two years earlier another business had expanded, adding Hispanic workers and their families to the McKay community. To respond to this community change, the McKay ISD had struggled to employ bilingual and English-As-a-Second Language (ESL) teachers and Spanish-speaking support staff. However, even now the district only employed one bilingual social worker, one bilingual principal, and the minimal number of bilingual and ESL teachers required by state standards. There were no bilingual counselors and no full-time trained Spanish translators.

Student achievement was being affected as evidenced by the results of the previous year's state-mandated achievement performance tests. For the first time since the test had been required, the district had gone from a Recognized District to Low Performing. This had been evident when the disaggregated test scores revealed less than satisfactory performance by Hispanic students. The number of Hispanic students in the district who had failed the test was not acceptable.

Superintendent Fletcher's pleasure at economic growth for the community was overshadowed by his awareness that the school district would be educating a growing Hispanic population that the district was poorly prepared to serve.

Subcommittee on Education

Just the past year, Superintendent Fletcher had formed a committee of school personnel, city and county government representatives, and other local leaders from diverse backgrounds to work with Dr. Ramon Torres, professor at Central State University, a regional university located in McKay, to study how the district might better serve its growing Hispanic population. Dr. Torres was particularly well suited to chair this committee because of his experience with bilingual programs and his work at the state education agency that had focused on the needs of Hispanic students and their families.

During the year, the subcommittee met with Hispanic parents and community members in a series of community forums. It made every effort to ensure that its work was inclusive, and it had been very thorough in its study. The subcommittee had reviewed data regarding the McKay ISD through the state education agency electronic database that included a district accountability summary, dropout data for grades 7–12, statewide assessment of academic skills indicator, and district data from 1994 to 2001.

Input from the Community

In the interviews, numerous Hispanic parents expressed concerns about their own and their children's inability to communicate with teachers and other school personnel due to language differences. There were a significant number of Hispanic adults who expressed motivation to learn English, get a high school diploma or GED, and even pursue postsecondary education. However, the committee learned that there were no agencies providing classes in Spanish on immigration issues, work permits, drivers' licenses, residency/citizenship, or voter registration in McKay.

Committee Recommendations

Dr. Torres, chair of the Subcommittee on Education, shared the findings with the City Commission, Superintendent Fletcher, and the school board. The Subcommittee on Education included the following recommendations:

- Recruit and hire more trained bilingual education and ESL teachers, as well as bilingual administrators, counselors, and social workers.
- Provide tuition assistance for bilingual instructional aides and support staff to attend community college or Central State University to become teachers.
- Ensure that McKay ISD strives to involve Hispanic parents in school activities.
- Implement a transportation plan to help the many students in poor neighborhoods who walk long distances to the bus stops because McKay ISD buses cannot travel the poorly maintained roads in inclement weather.
- Evaluate the efficacy of the ESL program in grades 7–12. The minimum of one class of ESL instruction per day required by state standards does not enable students to acquire the English proficiency they need to learn the advanced concepts being presented in English in all their other courses.
- Evaluate the efficacy of the preservice and inservice training being provided McKay ISD faculty and staff.
- Design curricula with consideration for Hispanic students.
- Address student and family conditions affecting student learning.

DISCUSSION TOPICS/QUESTIONS

1. What is the first step that Superintendent Fletcher and his administrative team should implement regarding the recommendations?
2. Construct an immediate plan for addressing needs of the new Hispanic students, as well as other LEP students already in the district.
3. What special programs within the district will be affected by these recommendations?
4. What community agencies might be available to help the district and in what ways? How can the district interface with other community agencies?
5. Identify strategies that will develop leadership capacity within this district.

6. If you were Superintendent Fletcher how would you demonstrate your growing sensitivity to multicultural issues in your district?
7. Develop a district plan for schools in McKay ISD to follow in identifying curriculum issues to be addressed.
8. Role-play a meeting between the superintendent and the two high school principals in the district. How would you help them create a Campus Plan based on the recommendations made by the Subcommittee on Education?
9. Evaluate your state's policies regarding bilingual education and ESL programs. What effect would these guidelines have on increasing or decreasing academic achievement of students who are not native English speakers?
10. Create a three-year plan for McKay ISD to once again become a Recognized School District.
11. How could Superintendent Fletcher involve Hispanic parents and/or community leaders in planning?

REFERENCES

Barth, R. (2002). The culture builder. *Educational Leadership, 59*(8), 6–11.
Cassity, J., and Harris, S. (2000). Parents of ESL students: A study of parental involvement. *National Association of Secondary School Principals Bulletin, 84*(619), 55–62.
Echols, C., and Stader, D. (2002). Education majors' attitudes about diversity. *Educational Leadership Review, 3*(2), 1–7.
Glickman, C. (2002). *Leadership for learning.* Alexandria, VA: Association for Supervision and Curriculum Development.
King, D. (2002). The changing shape of leadership. *Educational Leadership, 59*(8), 61–63.
Kuhlman, N., and Vidal, J. (1993). Meeting the needs of LEP students through teacher training: The case in California. *The Journal of Educational Issues of Language Minority Students, 12*, 98–99.
Mora, J. (2000). Staying the course in times of change: Preparing teachers for language minority education. *Journal of Teacher Education, 51*(5), 345–357.
Simmons, H. (1998). External agents, fostering multiculturalism. In *The multicultural campus: Strategies for transforming higher education* (pp.

51–68) Ed. L. A. Valverde and L. A. Castenell Jr., Walnut Creek, CA: Altmira Press.

U.S. Bureau of the Census. (1998). *Statistical abstract of the United States* (118th Ed.). Washington, DC.: U.S. Bureau of the Census.

ADDITIONAL RESOURCES

Delpit, L. (1995). *Other people's children: Cultural conflicts in the classroom.* New York: New Press.

Nieto, S. (1999). *The light in their eyes: Creating multicultural learning communities.* New York: Teachers College Press.

Nieto, S. (2000). *Affirming diversity: The sociopolitical context of multicultural education.* New York: Longman.

Paley, V. (2000). *White teacher.* Cambridge, MA: Harvard University Press.

Snow, M. A., ed. (2000). *Implementing the ESL standards for pre-K–12 students through teacher education.* Alexandria, VA: Teachers of Speakers of Other Languages.

Truscott, D., and Watts-Taffe, S. (2000). Using what we know about language and literacy development for ESL students in the mainstream classroom. *Language Arts, 77,* 258–265.

CHAPTER 7

Oops! Technology Problems

Texas Standard—Competency 007:

The superintendent knows how to implement a staff evaluation and development system to improve the performance of all staff members and select appropriate models for supervision and staff development.

ISLLC Standard 2:

A school administrator is an educational leader who promotes the success of all students by advocating, nurturing, and sustaining a school culture and instructional program conducive to student learning and staff professional growth.

NCATE Standard 2:

Candidates who complete the program are educational leaders who have the knowledge and ability to promote the success of all students by promoting a positive school culture, providing an effective instructional program, applying best practice to student learning, and designing comprehensive professional growth plans for staff.

ABSTRACT

The superintendent is responsible for leading his district in appropriate staff development, as well as securing outside resources to support the educational process. This case describes an experience of a superintendent who obtained a $4 million statewide technology improvement grant. Campuses underwent extensive modifications to accommodate the new equipment, and staff development was conducted. However, a year later, instead of improving campus morale and increasing district-wide use of technology, the superintendent discovered that staff morale was still low and, most disappointing of all, that the computer equipment was rarely used by faculty or by students.

OBJECTIVES

Objective 1: The superintendent knows how to develop, implement, and evaluate a professional development plan to address district needs.

Objective 2: The superintendent understands the role of technology in promoting student learning and professional growth.

Objective 3: The superintendent facilitates the application of adult learning principles to all professional development activities, including the use of support and follow-up strategies to facilitate implementation.

Objective 4: The superintendent knows how to diagnose organizational health and morale and implement strategies and programs to provide ongoing assistance and support to personnel.

LITERATURE REVIEW

While the push for schools to invest in more technology is supported by an increasing number of proponents, this movement is not without its opponents (Cooley, 2001). Certainly, many view computers as a key ingredient in educational reform, despite the cost of installation and maintenance. Yet others admit that technology is not "doing what we wish it to" (Bartles, 2000, p. 4). Still, a meta-analyses of research studies reported findings that computer-based instruction improved student learning, at least somewhat (Schacter and Fagnano, 1999). However, when Stratham and Torell (1996) review ten meta-analyses, they identify the necessary presence of two key components of effective technology programs for achievement gains for students. These components are proper implementation and appropriate use of computer technology.

In order for computer technology to be properly implemented and used appropriately in the schools, effective professional staff development is vital (Cooley, 2001). Unfortunately, too often, school districts spend huge amounts of money on technological materials, yet fail to develop effective teacher skills that will result in improved student learning (Moffitt, Friesma, and Brady, 1994). There is even widespread agreement that administrators are key players in the successful integration of technology into K–12 schools (Cooley and Reitz, 1997). To this end, administrators as well as teachers must learn about technology use in order to provide appropriate support within the district (Carr, 2001; Cooley, 2001).

In fact, faculty staff development and the use of technology have been identified as major components of school reform necessary for student success in the new millennium (Fullan and Hargreaves, 1996; U.S. Department of Education, 1994). Despite the important role of staff development in the successful implementation of technology planning, Sparks and Hirsh (1997) suggest that faculty professional development in most areas is still undeveloped and that school reform and teachers' professional development are seriously disconnected (Little, 1993).

In designing appropriate, effective staff development, adult learning principles must be at the very core. Principles that are necessary to facilitate adult learning identified by Brookfield (1986) include voluntary participation, mutual respect among participants and instructor, collaboration when setting objectives, activities and evaluating learning, and continuous reflection. An aim of staff development that is consistent with adult learning principles is the nurturing of self-direction and empowerment (Glickman, Gordon, and Ross-Gordon, 1998). Additionally, Schmoker (2001) recommends that a key motivator in establishing any program is frequent periodic short-term assessment.

According to Owen and Ovando (2000), the successful superintendent, in addition to other roles of politician and educator, must also be a wise manager. The first act of managerial leadership is interpersonal and involves the ability to supervise, the ability to control, the ability to coordinate, and the ability to represent. The second component of managerial leadership is informational, which includes the ability to inform and the ability to monitor. The third act of managerial leadership is decision making. This role includes the ability to analyze and organize and the ability to make firm decisions in a timely manner.

CASE STUDY

The Statewide Technology Improvement Grant

Superintendent Richard Lawrence knew that his district's technology plan was underserving the students and the faculty. However, he also knew that updating technology resources was a "black hole" in his budget, which was already tight. There was just no end to the demand for money in keeping technology current, even though many of the district campuses were less than fifteen years old.

When the eighteen-thousand-student population district of Springdale Consolidated School District (CSD) contracted with a grant writer's consortium at nearby Central State University to prepare a grant application for extensive technology updates, it had seemed a perfect solution to the district's technology needs. The final grant application included needs assessment, time-line, budget for software, as well as hardware, updated equipment, campus accommodations, student curricula, and faculty professional development for the early childhood through fifth grade campuses at Springdale CSD.

Superintendent Lawrence was thrilled when he heard the news that the $38 million grant was awarded. In fact, it was one of the largest grants awarded public school districts in the prior year's funding cycle. Each of the early childhood and elementary campuses was targeted for substantial infrastructure updates required to support new technology. Springdale CSD had moved quickly to complete necessary modifications to several of the older buildings at five elementary campuses. Computers were purchased for each classroom at the district's five early childhood and elementary campuses.

Professional Development

Funds for professional development were allocated through the grant, and professional development was scheduled by one of the companies that provided software. Installing the new equipment and training faculty had taken nearly an entire school year, but on several campuses, the training was now almost completed. Teachers were expected to begin using the new technology for computer-assisted instruction and for attendance, grade, and discipline reports at the beginning of the next school year. Additionally, many software programs had been purchased to supplement curriculum for student use in the classroom.

Yet teachers were complaining and very critical of the training provided them in using the new technology. In fact, evaluations of the professional development activities were critical of the presentations, and concerns were voiced from each of the five campuses that had completed the training. For the professional development training seminars the software providers had brought in graduate students from a nearby university who had no teaching experience, certainly no experience working with adult learners, to conduct the professional development sessions. The graduate students were described by several teachers as "condescending, impatient, computer geeks who had little or no interest in helping us master the material."

To make matters worse, the trainers had taught the newest version of software, but it was the older software that had been purchased and already loaded onto the computers. Thus, the training faculty had received did not match the software that was already loaded onto the computers.

The Meeting

The superintendent sat across from the five principals who looked accusingly at him. He could see on their faces that they blamed him. He knew that he had supported and encouraged the grant; however, *he* had not written the grant. And each of these principals had served on the committee. As superintendent he just could not do everything, or be everywhere, and technology was certainly not his specialty. How should he begin?

DISCUSSION TOPICS/QUESTIONS

1. How should Superintendent Lawrence begin this discussion with the campus principals?

2. How could the grant have been more effective in its implementation?
3. What are the components of an effective professional development model?
4. What are the components of an effective adult learning model?
5. Based on questions 3 and 4, construct an improved professional development plan for this district.
6. If you were one of the principals at the meeting, what recommendations would you make to the superintendent to help your campus at this point?
7. Identify a nearby school district that has had successful staff development. Interview the superintendent about his involvement in the process.
8. Construct a tool to evaluate the staff development program within your own district.

REFERENCES

Bartles, L. (2000). Gathering statistics: Is technology doing what you want it to? How do you know? Available online: www.electronic-school.com/2000/09/0900f5.html [accessed June 26, 2002].

Brookfield, S. (1986). *Understanding and facilitating adult learning*. San Francisco, CA: Jossey-Bass.

Carr, C. S. (2001). *New administrative connections: Technology, teaching, and learning*. Paper presented at the University Council of Educational Administrators annual conference, November 1–4, Cincinnati, Ohio.

Cooley, N. (2001). Instructional technology and improving student achievement. *The Informed Educator Series*. Arlington, VA: Educational Research Service.

Cooley, V. E., and Reitz, R. J. (1997). Lessons learned in creating a program. *Kappa Delta Pi, 34*(1), 4–9.

Fullan, M., and Hargreaves, A. (1996). *What's worth fighting for in your schools?* New York: Teachers College Press.

Glickman, C. D., Gordon, S. P., and Ross-Gordon, J. M. (1998). *Supervision of instruction: A developmental approach*. Boston, MA: Allyn & Bacon.

Little, J. (1993). Teachers' professional development in a climate of educational reform. *Education Evaluation and Policy Analysis, 15*(2), 129–159.

Moffitt, M., Friesma, J., and Brady, M. (1994). Bringing teachers up to speed. *Executive Educator,* 16–17, 47.

Owen, J., and Ovando, M. (2000). *Superintendent's guide to creating community.* Lanham, MD: Scarecrow Press.

Schacter, J., and Fagnano, C. (1999). Does computer technology improve student learning and achievement? How, when, and under what conditions? *Journal of Educational Computing Research, 20*(4), 329–343.

Schmoker, M. (2001). *The results fieldbook: Practical strategies from dramatically improved schools.* Alexandria, VA: Association for Supervision and Curriculum Development.

Sparks, D., and Hirsh, S. (1997). *A new vision for staff development.* Alexandria, VA: Association for Supervision and Curriculum Development.

Stratham, D., and Torell, C. (1996). *Computers in the classroom: The impact of technology on student learning.* Boise, ID: Army Research Institute, Boise State University College of Education.

U.S. Department of Education. (1994). *National goals report: Building a nation of learners.* Report by the National Educational Goals Panel. Washington, DC: U.S. Department of Education.

ADDITIONAL RESOURCES

Brewer, W. R., and Kallick, B. (1996). Technology's promise for reporting student learning. In *ASCD yearbook 1996: Communicating student learning* (pp. 178–187). Ed. T. Guskey. Alexandria, VA: Association for Supervision and Curriculum Development.

Fullan, M. (1993). *Change forces: Probing the depths of educational reform.* London., U.K.: Falmer Press.

Online website: www.electronic-school.com, editorially independent publication of the National School Boards Association.

Senge, P. et al. (2000). *Schools that learn: A fifth discipline fieldbook for educators, parents, and everyone who cares about education.* New York: Doubleday.

Vaughan, W. (2002). Professional development and the adoption and implementation of new innovations: Do teacher concerns matter? *International Electronic Journal for Leadership in Learning, 6*(5). Retrieved on March 25, 2002, from http://www.ucalgary.ca/~iejll/volme6/vaughan.html.

CHAPTER 8

Spending a Make-Believe Budget

Texas Standard—Competency 8:

The superintendent knows how to apply principles of effective leadership and management in relation to district budgeting, personnel, resource utilization, financial management, and technology use.

ISLLC Standard 3:

A school administrator is an educational leader who promotes the success of all students by ensuring management of the organization, operations, and resources for a safe, efficient, and effective learning environment.

NCATE 3:

Candidates who complete the program are educational leaders who have the knowledge and ability to promote the success of all students by managing the organization, operations, and resources in a way that promotes a safe, efficient, and effective learning environment.

ABSTRACT

An important role of the superintendent is to have the skills and abilities to manage the fiscal resources of the school district. At the same time, pressures brought about by greater demands for accountability exert powerful influences on educational leaders' ability to provide competent fiscal leadership and management. This case describes a district that was mired in a budget nightmare.

OBJECTIVES

Objective 1: The superintendent knows how to apply procedures for effective budget planning and management.

Objective 2: The superintendent knows how to work collaboratively with stakeholders to develop district budgets.

Objective 3: The superintendent facilitates effective account auditing and monitoring.

Objective 4: The superintendent establishes district procedures for accurate and effective purchasing and financial record keeping and reporting.

LITERATURE REVIEW

Today's pressures brought about by high taxes and the greater demands for accountability have powerful influences on educational leaders to provide competent fiscal leadership and management. Thus, a successful superintendent must have the skills and abilities to manage the fiscal resources of the school district in addition to myriad other roles that are also important to leading a successful organization (Thompson, Wood, and Honeyman, 1994).

Nearly fifty years ago, Eliot identified finance as one of the major content issues at the core of educational politics (1959). When resources are plentiful, conflicts can be easily overcome. However, when resources are scarce, superintendents often bear the brunt of unwise decisions, even if they were made by a predecessor. In fact, more superintendents lose jobs because of financial errors than all other issues (Owen and Ovando, 2001). Kowalski (1995), in his study of today's urban superintendents, reported one leader as saying that he would prefer being an instructional leader, but in reality, most of his time is spent managing and putting out fires.

The financing of schools itself is a very complicated issue and often the authority of superintendents appears undermined because many programs are paid for at least partially by state and federal funds that mandate certain requirements. Exacerbating this is the top-down pressure exerted by different levels of government and courts, and pressure from coalitions and other special interest groups at the local level (Kirst, 1984). Statewide revenue sources for schools include property taxes, state income taxes, local approved options, state foundation funding, and categorical assistance. Schools also have the issue of property wealth disparity, which is a contentious issue in most states (Sweetland and Maxwell, 2000).

Because of the importance of financial matters to superintendent success, often one of the first actions that many superintendents consider when they begin in a new district is the securing of adequate funding for initiatives that they anticipate proposing. While many superintendents spearhead bond elections, others have considered a new arena of fundraising that includes grants and gifts.

Superintendents interested in this type of funding should use the following techniques: form a local nonprofit education foundation, become familiar with fund-raising publications such as *The Chronicle of Philanthropy*, attend training workshops for fund-raising, and alert the local media about these efforts (Levinson, 2001). Corporate and foundation funding is a valuable source of funding for public schools today, though it is still underused. Even individual solicitations of major gifts can provide a significant source of outside funding for schools. These gifts can be of three types: annual campaign gifts, capital campaign gifts, and planned giving gifts (Levinson, 2001).

Recently, Public Agenda surveyed 853 school superintendents across the nation, and 66 percent complained that insufficient funding is a pressing problem in their districts. A major concern was that federal and state mandates often compel schools to offer certain services, yet 88 percent indicated that they rarely get "the resources necessary to fulfill them" (Johnson, 2002, p. 27). These superintendents also reported that they are required to use a "disproportional amount of money" for special education (p. 27). Despite these concerns, only 8 percent considered funding such a critical problem that it impeded progress. In other words, even though it is a problem, superintendents believe that they must make progress with the resources that they have.

CASE STUDY

New Leadership, New Policies and Procedures

When the Willington Independent School District Board (ISD) of Trustees finally adopted the annual budget in August, Superintendent

James Kilcullen had thought he could turn some of his attention to other matters for a few months. It had been a long, detailed, and often contentious budget process that had finally culminated in a budget that included not only significant improvements in technology but also an across-the-board pay increase for all employees.

The inner-city school district was faced with stagnant property values, slowly declining enrollment, and facilities and technology that were badly outdated. When Dr. Kilcullen became superintendent two years earlier, he knew that the Willington ISD faced many challenges and that the solution to most of these challenges would require increased spending on technology and renovations at several campuses.

Pay increases to keep pace with other school districts in and around the city were needed if the district was to be able to recruit and retain teachers when other nearby districts had starting salaries several thousand dollars higher than what Willington ISD was offering. These concerns were at least partially addressed in the new budget.

Changes in the Business Office

When Dr. Kilcullen became superintendent, he had promised the school board that he and his leadership team would bring about needed change in district budget and fiscal management procedures. He and other members of the Superintendent's Leadership Team had worked tirelessly, providing leadership for effective budget planning with involvement at each of the district's eighteen campuses. Numerous functions of the business office had been redefined with many new tasks delegated to the campuses. This process of "flattening" the administrative structure was one component of the Willington ISD Improvement Plan.

All faculty and staff members had not readily embraced this procedure, and several personnel changes in the district's business office had followed the retirement of longtime assistant superintendent for business Wayne Foster. While none of these personnel matters had been hostile, the retirements of experienced administrators and clerical staff in the business office had been followed by assignments of individuals with less experience than the retirees. As Foster remarked at his retirement party, "It's time to let some of you younger ones take over."

Planning the Budget

The budget planning process had started many months before the August school board meeting when it was adopted and had included extensive involvement at the campus and department levels. While each campus had not received all requests, this budget had been developed using a very different process than had ever been used in the Willington ISD.

The changes, along with extensive training of central office and campus leaders in effective financial record keeping, budgeting, purchasing, and reporting, had led to a management plan for acquiring, allocating, and managing resources according to the district's vision and priorities. Campus leaders were assigned additional management responsibilities, with financial, human, and material resources aligned to campus goals. Many budget decisions previously made at the central office level had been delegated to campuses. All campuses were held accountable for higher standards of student performance than ever before, and along with that accountability came necessary changes in the district's business policies and procedures.

"A budget is the district's instructional program written in numbers" had been the mantra as these changes were implemented. Although several critics had been quick to point out, "We've never done it that way before," the district had gone forward with the changes.

Developing the Budget

The increase in local taxes that was required to fund the budget had been the most challenging issue to work through with the school board. It had been especially difficult since the two newest board members, Annelle Young and John Reinhold, had campaigned on platforms that emphasized an extremely conservative philosophy and "no new taxes." Increased revenue from local taxes had been absolutely necessary because state per capita funding had decreased over the past years as enrollment had declined. Willington ISD depended on a combination of state funding, local tax revenue, and federal funding to meet the educational needs of its twenty-two thousand students.

When the school board adopted the budget and set a local tax rate sufficient to fund the budget, the board committed local taxpayers to a tax increase. The state funding system included incentives based on local tax collections, in effect rewarding school districts for setting higher local tax rates. Assistant superintendent for business Laura Scales had stressed in her report to the school board, "Local taxpayers have increasingly shouldered more of the burden. Now the state share of funding public schools is at a fifty-year low, and there's no place left to go for additional resources." Local taxes had to increase if state funding was to be maximized and a balanced budget sufficient to meet the district's needs was to be implemented.

Due to demographic changes in recent years, the student body was now 48 percent Hispanic, 37 percent African American, and 15 percent Anglo. Sixty-four percent of Willington ISD students were low socioeconomic, with many recent immigrants from Mexico. The number of students eligible for English-As-a-Second Language and Bilingual Education Programs had grown accordingly as these demographics developed.

These had not been simple issues to resolve, and Dr. Kilcullen had utilized many of the skills learned earlier in his previous position as deputy superintendent of the Spring Valley (ISD), a nearby suburban district. Campus-level expenditures, which had begun as "wish lists" from all eighteen campuses had been reduced significantly as draft versions of the budget were developed. Finally, after much discussion, a balanced budget, with expenditures equaling anticipated revenue, was unanimously adopted when the school board approved the superintendent's recommendation.

The Budget Nightmare

At first, Dr. Kilcullen simply could not believe what Scales had just told him. All eighteen Willington ISD campuses had received copies of the budget that *showed greater expenditures* in instructional technology, library and instructional materials, and extracurricular expenses than the budget finally approved by the school board. This early draft version had been entered into the district's financial management system and disseminated to all campuses. Every campus had spent through the fall accordingly, unaware that now almost all discretionary funds were depleted, just before the Christmas break.

When the error had been discovered early the previous morning, Scales and her staff had taken time to learn exactly what had happened before reporting to the superintendent. Expenditures, including encumbrances for items and services not yet received, far exceeded the correct budget, and this was only December. With over one-half of the school year remaining and most discretionary funds spent already, the district was in serious trouble. The correct budget had not been entered, but if it had been, it would have been badly overspent. The campuses were spending based on figures they had been provided in the draft copy of the budget. The problem was that the figures they had been provided were incorrect. A bigger problem was that almost all the money for the entire year was already spent!

DISCUSSION TOPICS/QUESTIONS

1. What is the first thing that Dr. Kilcullen and members of the Superintendent's Leadership Team could do to correct this problem?
2. Prepare a draft of Dr. Kilcullen's explanation to the school board.
3. Develop a statement appropriate for release to the local media.
4. What communication strategies would you suggest that Dr. Kilcullen follow to have maximum support of the community.
5. What steps would you use to solve the problem of the financial crisis?
6. Videotape an interview featuring the superintendent discussing the problem with a local news reporter.
7. What change would you make in policy to ensure that this type of mistake might not happen again?
8. Design a flow chart that accurately describes the budget adoption procedure.
9. Interview a local superintendent about finances.
10. Discuss the issue of disparity in state funding with property taxes. How would you create parity for high and low wealth districts?

REFERENCES

Eliot, T. (1959). Towards an understanding of public school politics. *American Political Science Review, 52,* 822–834.

Johnson, J. (2002). Staying ahead of the game. *Educational Leadership*, *59*(8), 26–30.

Kirst, M. (1984). *Who controls our schools? American values in conflict*. Stanford, CA: Stanford Alumni Association.

Kowalski, T. (1995). *Keepers of the flame: Contemporary urban superintendents*. Thousand Oaks, CA: Corwin Press.

Levinson, S. (2001). Moving a school district into big-time fund raising. *The School Administrator, 58*(11), 33.

Owen, J. and Ovando, M. (2001). *Superintendent's guide to creating community*. Lanham, MD: Scarecrow Press.

Sweetland, S., and Maxwell, R. (2000). Public policy challenges to the superintendency: School finance experiences from Ohio. *Education Leadership Review, 1*(3), 8–14.

Thompson, D., Wood, R., and Honeyman, D. (1994). *Fiscal leadership for schools*. White Plains, NY: Longman Publishing Group.

ADDITIONAL RESOURCES

Biddle, B., and Berliner, D. (2002). Unequal school funding in the United States. *Educational Leadership, 59*(8), 48–60.

Guzman, N., and Ramirez, A. (2000). Hard work makes good luck: A profile of success. In *Case studies of the superintendency* (pp. 97–104). Ed. P. Short and J. P. Scribner. Lanham, MD: Scarecrow Press.

Jones, E. (2002). *Cash management: A financial overview for school administrators*. Lanham, MD: Scarecrow Press.

CHAPTER 9

Contaminated Ground

Texas Standard—Competency 009:

The superintendent knows how to apply principles of leadership and management to the district's physical plant and support systems to ensure a safe and effective learning environment.

ISLLC Standard 3:

A school administrator is an educational leader who promotes the success of all students by ensuring management of the organization, operations, and resources for a safe, efficient, and effective learning environment.

NCATE Standard 3:

Candidates who complete the program are educational leaders who have the knowledge and ability to promote the success of all students by managing the organization, operations, and resources in a way that promotes a safe, efficient, and effective learning environment.

ABSTRACT

The management of resources includes more than just finances; it extends to all resources of the school, including property, plant, equipment, and transportation to name just a few. Providing a safe environment for students as well as all employees is a major part of utilizing resources appropriately. This district built transportation offices on the site of a former chemical plant. Now, employees are developing mysterious illnesses. How will the superintendent lead his district through this crisis?

OBJECTIVES

Objective 1: The superintendent knows how to implement strategies that enable the district's physical plant, equipment, and support systems to operate safely, efficiently, and effectively.

Objective 2: The superintendent is able to apply strategies for ensuring the safety of students and personnel and for addressing emergencies and security concerns.

Objective 3: The superintendent knows how to develop and implement procedures for crisis planning and for responding to crises.

Objective 4: The superintendent ensures that problems are confronted and resolved in a timely manner.

LITERATURE REVIEW

Owen and Ovando (2001) identify the governing board, vision, quality of education, and management of resources as significant issues contributing to either satisfaction or dissatisfaction with a superintendent. Because resources are limited, superintendents who demonstrate their knowledge and ability to manage all of the district's resources are much more apt to have the support of the community in their endeavors. In fact, a teacher commented, "There isn't quite the fight for the piece of cheese" (Owen and Ovando, 2001, p. 137). Clearly, effective resource management that focuses on educational excellence contributes to a positive community climate. However, when school resources (facilities and/or individuals) are threatened with harm from any number of sources, our response to crises must be specific and immediate.

There are many kinds of crises today that keep our schools from being safe. Some of these crises are *emerging,* and we can anticipate them and be prepared when they occur. Some of these crises are *ongoing.* But often, today, crises are *immediate*. We did not expect them, we were not prepared, yet how we respond communicates much about our organization (Bagin and Gallagher, 2001, p. 158). Most crisis plans should include the following:

1. Reasons for the plan.
2. The types of crises covered in the plan—a basic plan could range from a chemical spill to a school shooting.
3. Checklists for responding to each type of crises.
4. Procedures common to all crises—for example, seeing that students and staff are safe, contacting the appropriate authorities, informing the superintendent, establishing a chief spokesperson, dealing with the media, demonstrating concern, gathering necessary information, and reporting the facts.
5. Emergency telephone numbers.
6. Detailed maps of each school facility.
7. Procedural information—guidelines for closing school and evacuation procedures. (Bagin and Gallagher, 2001, pp. 158–159)

Another major component of any crisis plan should include an assessment system that gives valuable feedback on training, identifies ways to improve, identifies how to refine or redirect the plan, determines how to better budget for it, and helps ensure that individuals affected by the crisis were treated expeditiously and compassionately (Perea and Morrison, 1997).

Johnson, et al. (1997) suggest three components to keeping schools safe: 1) structuring cooperation at every organizational level of the school; 2) developing the ability to manage conflicts through problem solving and peer mediations; and 3) creating a culture that builds civic values. The school district in Albuquerque, New Mexico, for instance, has formed a District Critical Incident Response Team that takes the lead in planning and coordinating services for different types of crises.

This team is a coordinated, ongoing group that focuses on ensuring maximum safety and the emotional well-being of those involved; developing a district-wide crisis response plan; coordinating training needed to implement the plan; and collaborating with community agencies about how to communicate and the kinds of equipment and emergency supplies that might be needed (Perea and Morrison, 1997).

Although crisis plans should be developed as board-adopted policy, the superintendent and other campus leaders serve as a planning team to create the policy. However, it is the superintendent who is responsible for implementing the plan. This is an ideal time to involve community stakeholders, such as faculty, students, local agency representatives, and PTA representatives, in a collaborative team to keep the school safe. Crises can involve any number of incidents, which might include accidents, armed attack, bomb threats, fire, vandalism, chemical leaks, death of a student or faculty member, child abuse cases, and criminal indictment of a student or faculty member (Bagin and Gallagher, 2001).

CASE STUDY

Crisis at the Transportation Center

Bus driver Larry Blas had beaten cancer once. He did not want to face it again, but he was convinced that "something bad is happening at the transportation center." Fellow employees with him at the Grayson County Consolidated School District (CSD) Transportation Center were also suffering strange rashes and respiratory disorders, including two secretaries working inside the building. Many employees at the transportation center were wondering if their health problems were due to pesticides from the former Bowers Chemical Company that had once stood near the site of the new transportation center. They had heard a rumor that several workers had been ill with flu-like symptoms during construction of the transportation center.

When several transportation department employees met with their supervisor, Marty Whitaker, and the assistant superintendent, Dr. Janet Smith, sharing their worries about their health concerns, Dr. Smith immediately made plans to meet with Superintendent of Schools Dr. Paul Sammons. Blas told Whitaker and Dr. Smith that about thirty-five district workers had hired an attorney and were pushing for testing of their workplace. According to Blas, "Just after Christmas break, two of the maintenance department guys were doing some landscaping at the transportation center, and they could just smell something funny coming off the ground." Just as they were beginning their discussion about the crisis of unexplained health problems at the transportation center, Dr. Sammons' secretary interrupted them with an urgent telephone call from local physician Dr. Brian Jefferson.

Unexplained Illnesses

The superintendent and the young physician were friends. They were members of the same Rotary Club and, along with their families, were both active in the same church. This telephone conversation was not a social call; it was strictly business. Dr. Jefferson related that school bus driver Bill Atkins had just been hospitalized with severe respiratory distress and that bus driver Larry Blas was also ill, complaining of similar symptoms. Dr. Jefferson was in the process of contacting the State Environmental Protection Agency to make the agency aware of the health problems experienced by school district employees at the transportation center.

Before Dr. Sammons and Dr. Smith could summon other members of the superintendent's cabinet to share this frightening turn of events with them, Dr. Sammons took a telephone call from school board president Susan Larson. Larson worked as a registered nurse in a physician's office in the same building with Dr. Jefferson. She told the superintendent about the rumors of pesticide poisoning and toxic residue at the new J. L. Bowers Transportation Center.

The Gift of Land

The growing community of Monroe, population forty thousand, was the largest town in Grayson County and site of the school district administrative offices. The countywide school district served fifteen thousand students in the communities of Monroe, Brooksboro, Warren, Jackson, and Pugh. Located near the state capital in a southern state, the county's population was increasing rapidly due to relocation of several industries and its proximity to the state capital. New subdivisions had opened, bringing families with school-age children to the district. Grayson County was touted by realtors, civic organizations, and business leaders as a "wonderful place to live—away from the pollution of the city."

When Dr. Sammons accepted the superintendency three years earlier, a bond issue for construction of two new elementary schools, a ninth-grade center for the consolidated high school that served students from Brooksboro, Warren, and Jackson, and a transportation center had just been defeated by voters. Former superintendent Greg Burris had led the Grayson County CSD through nine years of rapid change and growth. Shortly after the defeated bond issue, he retired, and Dr. Sammons accepted the position of superintendent. Dr. Sammons immediately began work with the school district, community groups, and countywide committees to study the district's facility needs and to plan for another bond issue. When the bond issue passed, he and members of his staff were jubilant.

Planning for the new buildings began immediately after voters approved the bond issue. When the family of longtime school board member J. L. Bowers offered to donate fifty acres to the school district, the dilemma of where to build the new transportation center was resolved. Located just off State Highway 828, the fifty-acre plot was an ideal location, midway between Monroe and Brooksboro. The site had been unused for several years since a large chemical operation in California had bought the Bowers Chemical Company and relocated it out of state.

The school district gratefully accepted the gift of land and immediately began demolishing the existing structures to ready the property for construction. The new center, housing employees of the district's transportation department, with parking space for all the school buses and other district vehicles, was quickly built and opened. The J. L. Bowers Transportation Center was an important accomplishment.

Crisis Management

Dr. Sammons sat at his desk. Members of his administrative team were gathering in the adjoining conference room, speaking softly among themselves. Immediate action must be taken to ensure the safety and well-being of all students and personnel. The district's support system must be able to function safely, efficiently, and effectively. Applicable legal codes and all local, state, and federal regulations must be followed. But where should they begin?

DISCUSSION TOPICS/QUESTIONS

1. What will you do first? Support this action.
2. How will you involve the community in your actions?
3. What other community agencies will be involved in your crisis plan?

4. Develop a detailed plan of action for responding to this crisis. Include immediate, short-term, and long-range steps with specific responsibilities.

5. Identify other types of crises for which a school district must develop policies and procedures?

6. Evaluate your school policy and procedure manual for safe school policies.

7. Get together with other class members or superintendents and compare these policies.

8. Identify ways that your policy and procedure manual could be improved in this area.

9. If you were asked to determine important guidelines for making initial statements about crises, what might your guidelines be?

REFERENCES

Bagin, D., and Gallagher, D. (2001). *The school and community relations* (7th ed.). Boston, MA: Allyn & Bacon.

Johnson, D., et al. (1997). The three Cs of safe schools. *Educational Leadership, 55*(2), 8–13.

Owen, J., and Ovando, M. (2001). *Superintendent's guide to creating community.* Lanham, MD: Scarecrow Press.

Perea, R., and Morrison, S. (1997). Preparing for a crisis. *Educational Leadership, 55*(2), 42–44.

ADDITIONAL RESOURCES

Bagin, D., and Gallagher, D. (1993). *The Complete Crisis Communication Management Manual.* Rockville, MD: National School Public Relations.

Decker, R. H. (1997). *When a crisis hits: Will your school be ready?* Thousand Oaks, CA: Corwin Press.

Duke, D. (2002). *Creating safe schools for all children.* Boston, MA: Allyn & Bacon.

Dwyer, K., and Osher, D. (2000). *Safeguarding our children: An action guide.* Washington, DC: U.S. Departments of Education and Justice, American Institutes for Research.

CHAPTER 10

Accusations—True or False?

Texas Standard—Competency 010:

The superintendent knows how to apply organizational, decision-making, and problem-solving skills to facilitate positive change in varied contexts.

ISLLC Standard 1:

A school administrator is an educational leader who promotes the success of all students by facilitating the development, articulation, implementation, and stewardship of a vision of learning that is shared and supported by the school community.

NCATE Standard 1:

Candidates who complete the program are educational leaders who have the knowledge and ability to promote the success of all students by facilitating the development, articulation, implementation, and stewardship of a school or district vision of learning supported by the school community.

ABSTRACT

A major responsibility for a superintendent is to provide a safe environment for all faculty, as well as students. Superintendents must be skilled in appropriate decision making and problem solving in varied contexts. This case describes a situation where an administrator is accused of sexual harassment by a faculty member.

OBJECTIVES

Objective 1: The superintendent knows how to implement processes for gathering, analyzing, and using data for informed decision making.

Objective 2: The superintendent knows how to frame, analyze, and resolve problems using appropriate problem-solving techniques and decision-making skills.

Objective 3: The superintendent ensures that the core beliefs of the school vision are modeled for all stakeholders.

Objective 4: The superintendent knows how to use appropriate interpersonal skills in a variety of situations.

LITERATURE REVIEW

Sexual harassment is the most common allegation of sexual discrimination in schools. While federal law does not prohibit sexual harassment specifically, it defines sexual harassment as a form of sex discrimination. Federal guidelines define sexual harassment as "unwelcome sexual advances, requests for sexual favors, and other verbal or physical conduct of a sexual nature" where "conduct has the purpose or effect of unreasonably interfering with an individual's work performance or creating an intimidating, hostile or offensive working environment" (29 C.F.R. §1604.11(a)). These cases are divided into two categories: quid pro quo—where there is an actual trade off, such as promotion—and hostile environment—where unwelcome sexual advances create an offensive environment (Kemerer and Walsh, 1996).

Title IX of the 1972 Education Amendments prohibits intentional discrimination on the basis of sex in any program that receives federal assistance. In 1982, the U.S. Supreme Court ruled in *North Haven Board of Education v. Bell* that Title IX applied to employees as well as students. Although with the U.S. Supreme Court's 1992 decision upholding the right of student victims to sue for compensatory damages (*Franklin v. Gwinnett County Public Schools*, 1992), Title IX may not be used as an avenue for the recovery of damages for employees. Instead, employees of federally funded educational institutions who seek money damages must file their claims through Title VII rather than Title IX. This ruling means that sexual harassment claims must be subjected to the administrative process required under Title VII before a suit can be filed (Kemerer and Walsh, 1996).

A leader's image is generally created when beliefs and practices come together in decision making as the leader focuses on critical issues that help or inhibit the school district in its functioning. However, Farson (2002) interviewed CEOs discovered that most made only a "few really important decisions in a year and then only after prodigious research and consultation and soul searching" (p. 6). Instead, leaders of organizations spend most of their time talking to people and, it is in this way that they "put out fires" and keep the organization together.

Too often decision making and problem solving are considered to be the same. But Farson (2002) suggested that as leaders move up the ladder of responsibility, they deal with fewer problems (specific happenings that can be analyzed and solved) and more predicaments (permanent, complex dilemmas). Thus, issues faced by school leaders are generally predicaments where the top leader must make decisions that allow the organization to "cope" with circumstances rather than solve issues with a sense of finality.

Hoy and Miskel (2001) identified five action steps in the decision-making process. These steps are to 1) recognize and define the problem; 2) analyze the difficulties in the situation; 3) establish criteria for a satisfactory solution; 4) develop an action plan; and 5) initiate the plan. They also point out that there are many decision strategies, such as classical (ends are determined, and then the means to obtain them), administrative (means-ends analysis, with ends occasionally changing), incremental (cannot separate the means from the ends), and mixed scanning (focuses on broad ends with tentative means). However, it is most important for a leader to be able to match the right decision strategies with changing circumstances (Hoy and Miskel, 2001).

Organizational management can take many forms within a district. However, when superintendents work to make decisions (and problem solve) that build leadership capacity within the district and community, the following conditions need to be created:

1. Hire personnel with proven capacity to do the work of a leader;
2. Build relationships that are trusting;

3. Assess the faculty capacity for doing the work of leadership;
4. Develop a culture of inquiry that reflects, questions, gathers information, and plans for improvement;
5. Establish inclusive, collaborative governance structures;
6. Anticipate changes in individual roles and provide professional development;
7. Develop district policies and procedures that support the work of leadership. (Lambert, 1998, p. 19)

Goldman (1998) suggested that in order to know the essence of the school leader, it is only necessary to look at the tone and educational environment of the organization. This is consistent with findings by Smart and St. John (1996) who suggest that strong organizational cultures are most effective when there is a congruence between stated beliefs and actual practices.

CASE STUDY

Changes at Cedillo High School

Cedillo High School principal James Stephenson had led an intensive restructuring of the sprawling 2,280-student, ethnically and racially diverse campus over the past three years. According to all student success indicators, the campus was making significant gains on the state assessments for nine- and tenth-grade students. Scores in mathematics, language arts, writing, social studies, and science had improved each year of his leadership. And despite the predominantly at-risk student population served at Cedillo High School, the dropout rate was lower than state averages,

Curriculum development and alignment projects had resulted in Advanced Placement courses being offered this year for the first time. Additionally, several low-level courses, such as Fundamentals of Mathematics, had been replaced by higher level, more challenging courses. The campus focus on instructional improvement was apparent.

James Stephenson's Leadership Style

Principal James Stephenson had graduated with honors from Cedillo High School himself. A star athlete in high school and college, his career as a professional football player had ended due to an injury soon after he was drafted. When he returned to his hometown to teach high school mathematics, he quickly moved through the ranks to become a middle school principal before being assigned to his alma mater, Cedillo High School. His warm, friendly personality was heralded by his supporters as exactly what was needed to lead Cedillo High School. One of only two African American administrators in the district, he was rapidly acknowledged as a leader in community and civic affairs, as well as within the ranks of school district teachers and administrators.

As he began to lead the faculty in site-based decision making, curriculum development, and other projects dedicated to improving student performance, he was frequently heard to say, "We don't take excuses at this school. These kids can learn and we will give them every opportunity to be successful."

His critics had complained that he was moving too quickly and that he fostered unreal expectations. Several longtime faculty members retired and several others requested and were granted transfers to another high school in the same district. While he was generally supported by parents and community members, there was a contingent of Cedillo High School faculty who were becoming more vocal in their criticisms of Mr. Stephenson's leadership. Several teachers had complained that he showed favoritism among the teachers and that he simply would not listen to faculty concerns.

Kay Jackson's Story

Dr. John Martindale, superintendent of the Cedillo Independent School District, had just met with the assistant superintendent for human resources Julia Warren, the assistant superintendent Juan Martinez, and the high school language arts teacher Kay Jackson in his office. Ms. Jackson had scheduled the conference earlier that morning when she telephoned Ms. Warren to say that she was resigning immediately unless changes were made at Cedillo High School.

According to Ms. Jackson, Mr. Stephenson had been making inappropriate remarks to her for several months. She told Dr. Martindale, Ms. Warren, and Mr. Martinez that Mr. Stephenson had always been friendly and interested in her when she joined the Cedillo High School faculty two years earlier. He had made a point of encouraging her innovative teaching strategies and her work with student organizations.

When her husband had been deployed as a member of the National Guard in early February, Ms. Jackson had suddenly been faced with total responsibility for herself and their two preschool children. Since her family lived two hundred miles away, she and the children were without family support in Cedillo. Mr. Stephenson had arranged for his teenage daughter, Sabrina, to baby-sit when Ms. Jackson was involved with school functions during the evenings and had offered her a ride to school when her car was in the shop for repairs.

Ms. Jackson related that her principal's thoughtfulness and offers to help had taken a different turn recently. He had begun complimenting her dress and appearance, telling her that she looked pretty and that certain outfits were especially flattering. He had joined her at lunch in the faculty lounge several times recently and had made her uncomfortable by his comments, asking how she was managing without a man around the house and speculating that she must be "pretty lonely."

In tears, Ms. Jackson told the superintendent and the two assistant superintendents that the previous afternoon she had stayed at school until 4:45, working in her classroom grading papers and averaging grades for the end of the grading period. She related that Mr. Stephenson came into her classroom where she was working alone at her desk. He asked her to meet him that night at the school, noting that she could get his daughter, Sabrina, to stay with her children for a few hours. According to Ms. Jackson, he told her, "I'm really attracted to you and it won't hurt anyone if you and I get better acquainted. Your husband is half way around the world and my wife is so busy she won't notice."

According to Ms. Jackson, she was ready to resign and move closer to her family because the other teachers had noticed the attention he was paying her and were gossiping about it. She related that she was afraid to remain at Cedillo High School, "My husband will be back and I still want to be married to him. He'll be furious when he hears about all this gossip."

Other Sides of the Story

Dr. Martindale knew that an immediate investigation was necessary. He telephoned Cedillo High School and arranged to meet with Mr.

Stephenson at 4:00 that afternoon. Mr. Stephenson told Dr. Martindale that he knew what the conference was about, and he was "ready to clear this whole thing up." He added, "This is all about some teachers not wanting to do their jobs and their efforts to discredit me and the good things we're doing for kids at the high school."

Before the 4:00 meeting with Mr. Stephenson, Dr. Martindale had accepted telephone calls from three high school teachers who shared their thoughts on the rumors that were rampant at the high school. One veteran teacher, Shirley Jenkins, was particularly outspoken and demanded to know what was going to be done about the "disgraceful situation" at the high school. She told Dr. Martindale, "Everyone at our campus knows they're having an affair. Students are watching her house trying to catch them together there."

Another longtime Cedillo High School teacher Maria Ramirez told the superintendent that Principal Stephenson should be forced to resign immediately. She described him as a well-known "ladies man" who was not morally fit to lead the school.

High school mathematics teacher Elizabeth Phillips had a different perspective when she called the superintendent, "There's a lot of talk going around right now and it needs to stop. Every time Kay Jackson tells her story, it gets more lurid. She needs to teach her classes and stop the soap opera stuff." Although Ms. Phillips didn't reveal the names of the other teachers who shared her perspective, she did indicate that there were several other teachers who agreed with her.

The Superintendent's Responsibility

At 3:45 that afternoon, Dr. Martindale waited for his friend James Stephenson to arrive for their conference. Dr. Martindale had encouraged Mr. Stephenson to apply for the Cedillo High School principalship and had strongly supported his efforts to improve academics.

DISCUSSION TOPICS/QUESTIONS

1. What would be the initial step(s) for Dr. Martindale to take?
2. What legal issues must be considered in an alleged harassment situation?

3. How and what should Dr. Martindale communicate to the school board about the alleged sexual harassment?
4. What should the superintendent say to Cedillo High School students, parents, and faculty about this situation?
5. Prepare a statement to release to the media about the allegations.
6. Review and summarize your district's sexual harassment policy.
7. Regarding the policy of decision making, how are decisions made in your district, and who ultimately makes such decisions? Construct a graphic that depicts decision making in your district.
8. How would you distinguish between problems and predicaments (see Farson, 2002)? What problems do you think that superintendents face? What predicaments do they face?

REFERENCES

Farson, R. (2002). Decisions, dilemmas, and dangers. *The School Administrator, 59*(2), 6–13.
Franklin v. Gwinnett County Public Schools. (1992). 112 S. Ct. 1028.
Goldman, E. (1998). The significance of leadership style. *Educational Leadership, 55*(7), 20–22.
Hoy, W., and Miskel, C. (2001). *Educational administration: Theory, research, and practice* (6th ed.). Boston, MA: McGraw-Hill.
Kemerer, F., and Walsh, J. (1996). *The educator's guide to Texas school law* (4th ed.). Austin, TX: University of Texas Press.
Lambert, L. (1998). How to build leadership capacity. *Educational Leadership, 55*(7), 17–19.
Smart, J. C., and St. John, E. P. (1996). Organizational culture and effectiveness in higher education: A test of the Culture Type and Strong Culture Hypotheses. *Educational Evaluation and Policy Analysis, 18*(3), 219–241.

ADDITIONAL RESOURCES

Adams, N., and McCormick, J. (1999, Fall). Legal and ethical considerations for school administrators. *Insight, 13*(3), 12–14.
Horner, J., and Singleton, M. (1999, Fall). School tort liability and governmental/official immunity. *Insight, 13*(3), 25–30.
Kowalski, T. (2001). *Case studies on educational administration* (3rd ed.). New York: Longman.

Norton, M., Webb, L., Dlugosh, L., and Sybouts, W. (1996). *The school superintendency: New responsibilities, new leadership*. Boston, MA: Allyn & Bacon.

Spillane, R., and Regnier, P. (1998). *The superintendent of the future: Strategy and action for achieving academic excellence*. Gaithersburg, MD: Aspen Publishers.

Yudof, M., et al. (2002). *Educational policy and the law* (4th ed.). Belmont, CA: Wadsworth Group/Thomson Learning.

Texas Competencies for the Superintendent

DOMAIN I—LEADERSHIP OF THE EDUCATIONAL COMMUNITY

Competency 001

The superintendent knows how to act with integrity, with fairness, and in an ethical manner in order to promote the success of all students. The superintendent knows how to

- serve as an advocate for all children
- model and promote the highest standard of conduct, ethical principles, and integrity in decision making, actions, and behaviors
- implement policies and procedures that promote district personnel compliance with The Code of Ethics and Standard Practices for Texas Educators
- apply knowledge of ethical issues affecting education
- apply laws, policies, and procedures in a fair and reasonable manner
- interact with district staff and students in a professional manner

Competency 002

The superintendent knows how to shape district culture by facilitating the development, articulation, implementation, and stewardship of a vision of learning that is shared and supported by the educational community.

---

*Available: www.sbec.state.tx.us
Retrieved online: www.sbec.state.tx.us on June 28, 2002—State Board of Educator Certification.

The superintendent knows how to

- establish and support a district culture that promotes learning, high expectations, and academic rigor for self, students, and staff.
- facilitate the development and implementation of a shared vision that focuses on teaching and learning and ensures the success of all students.
- implement strategies for involving all stakeholders in planning processes and for facilitating planning between constituencies.
- use formal and informal techniques to monitor and assess district/school climate for effective, responsive decision making.
- institute procedures for monitoring the accomplishment of district goals and objectives to achieve the district's vision.
- facilitate the development, use, and allocation of all available resources, including human resources, to support implementation of the district's vision and goals.
- recognize and celebrate contributions of staff and community toward realization of the district's vision.
- maintain awareness of emerging issues and trends affecting public education and communicate their significance to the local educational community.
- encourage and model innovative thinking and risk taking and view problems as learning opportunities.
- promote multicultural awareness, gender sensitivity, and the appreciation of diversity in the educational community.

Competency 003

The superintendent knows how to communicate and collaborate with families and community members, respond to diverse community interests and needs, and mobilize community resources to ensure educational success for all students.

The superintendent knows how to

- serve as an articulate spokesperson for the importance of public education in a free democratic society.

- develop and implement an effective and comprehensive internal and external district communications plan and public relations program.
- analyze community and district structures and identify major opinion leaders and their relationships to district goals and programs.
- establish partnerships with families, area businesses, institutions of higher education, and community groups to strengthen programs and to support district goals.
- implement effective strategies for systematically communicating with and gathering input from all stakeholders in the district.
- communicate and work effectively with diverse social, cultural, ethnic, and racial groups in the district and community so that all students receive appropriate resources and instructional support to ensure educational success.
- develop and use formal and informal techniques to gain an accurate view of the perceptions of district staff, families, and community members.
- use effective consensus-building and conflict-management skills.
- articulate the district's vision and priorities to the community and to the media.
- influence the media by using proactive communication strategies that serve to enhance and promote the district's vision.
- communicate effectively about positions on educational issues.
- use effective and forceful writing, speaking, and active listening skills.

Competency 004

The superintendent knows how to respond to and influence the larger political, social, economic, legal, and cultural context, including working with the board of trustees, to achieve the district's educational vision.

The superintendent knows how to

- analyze and respond to political, social, economic, and cultural factors affecting students and education.

- provide leadership in defining superintendent–board roles and establishing mutual expectations.
- communicate and work effectively with board members in varied contexts, including problem-solving and decision-making contexts.
- work with the board of trustees to define mutual expectations, policies, and standards.
- access and work with local, state, and national political systems and organizations to elicit input on critical educational issues.
- use legal guidelines to protect the rights of students and staff and to improve learning opportunities.
- prepare and recommend district policies to improve student learning and district performance in compliance with state and federal requirements.

DOMAIN II—INSTRUCTIONAL LEADERSHIP

Competency 005

The superintendent knows how to facilitate the planning and implementation of strategic plans that enhance teaching and learning; ensure alignment among curriculum, curriculum resources, and assessment; and promote the use of varied assessments to measure student performance.

The superintendent knows how to

- facilitate effective curricular decision making based on an understanding of pedagogy, curriculum design, cognitive development, learning processes, and child and adolescent growth and development.
- implement planning procedures to develop curricula that achieve optimal student learning and that anticipate and to respond to occupational and economic trends.
- implement core curriculum design and delivery systems to ensure instructional quality and continuity across the district.
- develop and implement collaborative processes for systematically assessing and renewing the curriculum to meet the needs of all students and ensure appropriate scope, sequence, content, and alignment.

- use assessment to measure student learning and to diagnose student needs to ensure educational accountability.
- evaluate district curricula and provide direction for improving curricula based on sound, research-based practices.
- integrate the use of technology, telecommunications, and information systems into the school district curriculum to enhance learning for all students.
- facilitate the use of creative thinking, critical thinking, and problem solving by staff and other school district stakeholders involved in curriculum design and delivery.
- facilitate the effective coordination of district and campus curricular and extracurricular programs.

Competency 006

The superintendent knows how to advocate, nurture, and sustain an instructional program and a district culture that are conducive to student learning and staff professional growth.

The superintendent knows how to

- apply knowledge of motivational theories to create conditions that encourage staff, students, families/caregivers, and the community to strive to achieve the district's vision.
- facilitate the implementation of sound, research-based theories and techniques of classroom management, student discipline, and school safety to ensure a school district environment conducive to learning.
- facilitate the development of a learning organization that encourages educational excellence, supports instructional improvement, and incorporates best practice.
- facilitate the ongoing study of current best practice and relevant research and encourage the application of this knowledge to district/school improvement initiatives.
- plan and manage student services and activity programs to address developmental, scholastic, social, emotional, cultural, physical, and leadership needs.

- establish a comprehensive school district program of student assessment, interpretation of data, and reporting of state and national data results.
- apply knowledge of special programs to ensure that students with special needs are provided with appropriate resources and effective, flexible instructional programs and services.
- analyze instructional resource needs and deploy instructional resources effectively and equitably to enhance student learning.
- analyze the implications of various organizational factors (e.g., staffing patterns, class scheduling formats, school organizational structures, student discipline practices) for teaching and learning.
- develop, implement, and evaluate change processes to improve student and adult learning and the climate for learning.
- ensure responsiveness to diverse sociological, linguistic, cultural, psychological, and other factors that may affect student development and learning and create an environment in which all students can learn.

Competency 007

The superintendent knows how to implement a staff evaluation and development system to improve the performance of all staff members and select appropriate models for supervision and staff development.

The superintendent knows how to

- enhance teaching and learning by participating in quality professional development activities and by studying current professional literature and research.
- develop, implement, and evaluate a comprehensive professional development plan to address identified areas of district, campus, and/or staff need.
- facilitate the application of adult learning principles to all professional development activities, including the use of support and follow-up strategies to facilitate implementation.
- implement strategies to enhance professional capabilities at the district and campus level.

- work collaboratively with other district personnel to plan, implement, and evaluate professional growth programs.
- deliver effective presentations and facilitate learning for both small and large groups.
- implement effective strategies for the recruitment, selection, induction, development, evaluation, and promotion of staff.
- develop and implement comprehensive staff evaluation models that include both formative and summative assessment and appraisal strategies.
- diagnose organizational health and morale and implement strategies and programs to provide ongoing assistance and support to personnel.

DOMAIN III—ADMINISTRATIVE LEADERSHIP

Competency 008

The superintendent knows how to apply principles of effective leadership and management in relation to district budgeting, personnel, resource utilization, financial management, and technology use.

The superintendent knows how to

- apply procedures for effective budget planning and management.
- work collaboratively with stakeholders to develop district budgets.
- facilitate effective account auditing and monitoring.
- establish district procedures for accurate and effective purchasing and financial record keeping and reporting.
- acquire, allocate, and manage resources according to district vision and priorities, including obtaining and using funding from various sources.
- use district and staff evaluation data for personnel policy development and decision making.
- apply knowledge of certification requirements and standards.
- apply knowledge of legal requirements associated with personnel management, including requirements relating to recruiting, screening, selecting, evaluating, disciplining, reassigning, and dismissing personnel.

- manage one's own time and the time of others to maximize attainment of district goals.
- develop and implement plans for using technology and information systems to enhance school district operations.
- apply pertinent legal concepts, regulations, and codes.

Competency 009

The superintendent knows how to apply principles of leadership and management to the district's physical plant and support systems to ensure a safe and effective learning environment.

The superintendent knows how to

- apply procedures for planning, funding, renovating, and/or constructing school facilities.
- implement strategies that enable the district's physical plant, equipment, and support systems to operate safely, efficiently, and effectively.
- apply strategies for ensuring the safety of students and personnel and for addressing emergencies and security concerns.
- develop and implement procedures for crisis planning and for responding to crises.
- apply procedures for ensuring the effective operation and maintenance of district facilities.
- implement appropriate, effective procedures in relation to district transportation services, food services, health services, and other services.
- apply pertinent legal concepts, regulations, and codes.

Competency 010

The superintendent knows how to apply organizational, decision-making, and problem-solving skills to facilitate positive change in varied contexts.

The superintendent knows how to

- implement appropriate management techniques and group process skills to define roles, assign functions, delegate effectively, and determine accountability for goal attainment.
- implement processes for gathering, analyzing, and using data for informed decision making.
- frame, analyze, and resolve problems using appropriate problem-solving techniques and decision-making skills.
- use strategies for working with others, including the board of trustees, to promote collaborative decision making and problem solving, facilitate team building, and develop consensus.
- encourage and facilitate positive change, enlist support for change, and overcome obstacles to change in varied educational contexts.
- apply skills for monitoring and evaluating change and making needed adjustments to achieve goals.
- analyze and manage internal and external political systems to benefit the educational organization.

Standards for School Leaders

INTERSTATE SCHOOL LEADERS LICENSURE CONSORTIUM STANDARDS

The Interstate School Leaders Licensure Consortium (ISLLC) Standards have recently been developed by the Council of Chief State School Officers in collaboration with the National Policy Board on Educational Administration (NPBEA). There are six standards. Each standard is followed by the *Knowledge* required for the standard, the *Dispositions* or attitudes manifest by the accomplishment of the standard, and *Performances* that could be observed by an administrator who is accomplished in the standard.

Standard 1

A school administrator is an educational leader who promotes the success of all students by facilitating the development, articulation, implementation, and stewardship of a vision of learning that is shared and supported by the school community.

Knowledge. The administrator has knowledge and understanding of

- learning goals in a pluralistic society
- the principles of developing and implementing strategic plans
- systems theory
- information sources, data collection, and data analysis strategies

---

*Retrieved online: www.ccsso.org/standards on December 12, 2001.

- effective communication
- effective consensus-building and negotiation skills

Dispositions. The administrator believes in, values, and is committed to

- the educability of all
- a school vision of high standards of learning
- continuous school improvement
- the inclusion of all members of the school community
- ensuring that students have knowledge, skills, and values to become successful adults
- a willingness to continuously examine one's own assumptions, beliefs, and practices
- doing the work required for high levels of personal and organizational performance

Performances. The administrator facilitates processes and engages in activities ensuring that

- the vision and school mission are effectively communicated to staff, parents, students, and community members
- the vision and mission are communicated through the use of symbols, ceremonies, stories, and similar activities
- the core beliefs of the school vision are modeled for all stakeholders
- the vision is developed with and among stakeholders
- the contributions of school community members to the realization of the vision are recognized and celebrated
- the progress toward the vision and mission is communicated to all stakeholders
- the school community is involved in school improvement efforts
- the vision shapes the educational programs, plans, and actions
- an implementation plan is developed in which objectives and strategies to achieve the vision and goals are clearly articulated
- the assessment data related to student learning are used to develop the school vision and goals

- the relevant demographic data pertaining to students and to their families are used in developing the school mission and goals
- the barriers to achieving the vision are identified, clarified, and addressed
- the needed resources are sought and obtained to support the implementation of the school mission and goals
- the existing resources are used in support of the school vision and goals
- the vision, mission, and implementation plans are regularly monitored, evaluated, revised

Standard 2

A school administrator is an educational leader who promotes the success of all students by advocating, nurturing, and sustaining a school culture and instructional program conducive to student learning and staff professional growth.

Knowledge. The administrator has knowledge and understanding of

- student growth and development
- applied learning theories
- applied motivational theories
- curriculum design, implementation, evaluation, and refinement
- principles of effective instruction
- measurement, evaluation, and assessment strategies
- diversity and its meaning for educational programs
- adult learning and professional development models and the change process for systems, organizations, and individuals
- the role of technology in promoting student learning and professional growth
- school cultures

Dispositions. The administrator believes in, values, and is committed to

- student learning as the fundamental purpose of schooling
- the proposition that all students can learn

- the variety of ways in which students can learn
- lifelong learning for self and others
- professional development as an integral part of school improvement
- the benefits that diversity brings to the school community
- a safe and supportive learning environment
- preparing students to be contributing members of society

Performances. The administrator facilitates processes and engages in activities ensuring that

- all individuals are treated with fairness, dignity, and respect
- professional development promotes a focus on student learning consistent with the school vision and goals
- students and staff feel valued and important
- the responsibilities and contributions of each individual are acknowledged
- barriers to student learning are identified, clarified, and addressed
- diversity is considered in developing learning experiences
- lifelong learning is encouraged and modeled
- there is a culture of high expectations for self, student, and staff performance
- technologies are used in teaching and learning
- student and staff accomplishments are recognized and celebrated
- multiple opportunities to learn are available to all students
- the school is organized and aligned for success
- curricular, cocurricular, and extracurricular programs are designed, implemented, evaluated, and refined
- curriculum decisions are based on research, expertise of teachers, and the recommendations of learned societies
- the school culture and climate are assessed on a regular basis
- a variety of sources of information are used to make decisions
- student learning is assessed using a variety of techniques
- multiple sources of information regarding performance are used by staff and students
- a variety of supervisory and evaluation models are employed
- pupil personnel programs are developed to meet the needs of students and their families

Standard 3

A school administrator is an educational leader who promotes the success of all students by ensuring management of the organization, operations, and resources for a safe, efficient, and effective learning environment.

Knowledge. The administrator has knowledge and understanding of

- theories and models of organizations and the principles of organizational development
- operational procedures at the school and district level
- principles and issues relating to school safety and security
- human resources management and development
- principles and issues relating to fiscal operations of school management
- principles and issues relating to school facilities and use of space
- legal issues having an impact on school operations
- current technologies that support management functions

Dispositions. The administrator believes in, values, and is committed to

- making management decisions to enhance learning and teaching
- taking risks to improve schools
- trusting people and their judgments
- accepting responsibility
- high-quality standards, expectations, and performances
- involving stakeholders in management processes
- a safe environment

Performances. The administrator facilitates processes and engages in activities ensuring that

- knowledge of learning, teaching, and student development is used to inform management decisions
- operational procedures are designed and managed to maximize opportunities for successful learning
- emerging trends are recognized, studied, and applied as appropriate

- operational plans and procedures to achieve the vision and goals of the school are in place
- collective bargaining and other contractual agreements related to the school are effectively managed
- the school plant, equipment, and support systems operate safely, efficiently, and effectively
- time is managed to maximize attainment of organizational goals
- potential problems and opportunities are identified
- problems are confronted and resolved in a timely manner
- financial, human, and material resources are aligned to the goals of schools
- the school acts entrepreneurially to support continuous improvement
- organizational systems are regularly monitored and modified as needed
- stakeholders are involved in decisions affecting schools
- responsibility is shared to maximize ownership and accountability
- effective problem-framing and problem-solving skills are used
- effective conflict resolution skills are used
- effective group-process and consensus-building skills are used
- effective communication skills are used
- a safe, clean, and aesthetically pleasing school environment is created and maintained
- human resource functions support the attainment of school goals
- confidentiality and privacy of school records are maintained

Standard 4

A school administrator is an educational leader who promotes the success of all students by collaborating with families and community members, responding to diverse community interests and needs, and mobilizing community resources.

Knowledge. The administrator has knowledge and understanding of

- emerging issues and trends that potentially have an impact on the school community
- the conditions and dynamics of the diverse school community
- community resources

- community relations and marketing strategies and processes
- successful models of school, family, business, community, government, and higher education partnerships

Dispositions. The administrator believes in, values, and is committed to:

- schools operating as an integral part of the larger community
- collaboration and communication with families
- involvement of families and other stakeholders in school decision-making processes
- the proposition that diversity enriches the school
- families as partners in the education of their children
- the proposition that families have the best interests of their children in mind
- resources of the family and community needing to be brought to bear on the education of students
- an informed public

Performances. The administrator facilitates processes and engages in activities ensuring that

- high visibility, active involvement, and communication with the larger community is a priority
- relationships with community leaders are identified and nurtured
- information about family and community concerns, expectations, and needs is used regularly
- there is outreach to different business, religious, political, and service agencies and organizations
- credence is given to individuals and to groups whose values and opinions may conflict
- the school and community serve one another as resources
- available community resources are secured to help schools solve problems and achieve goals
- partnerships are established with area businesses, institutions of higher education, and community groups to strengthen programs and to support school goals

- community youth family services are integrated with school programs
- community stakeholders are treated equitably
- diversity is recognized and valued
- effective media relations are developed and maintained
- a comprehensive program of community relations is established
- public resources and funds are used appropriately and wisely
- community collaboration is modeled for staff
- opportunities for staff to develop collaborative skills are provided

Standard 5

A school administrator is an educational leader who promotes the success of all students by acting with integrity, with fairness, and in an ethical manner.

Knowledge. The administrator has knowledge and understanding of

- the purpose of education and the role of leadership in modern society
- various ethical frameworks and perspectives on ethics
- the values of the diverse school community
- professional codes of ethics
- the philosophy and history of education

Dispositions. The administrator believes in, values, and is committed to

- the ideal of the common good
- the principles in the Bill of Rights
- the right of every student to a free, quality education
- bringing ethical principles to the decision-making process
- subordinating one's own interest to the good of the school community
- accepting the consequences for upholding one's principles and actions
- using the influence of one's office constructively and productively in the service of all students and their families
- development of a caring school community

Performances. The administrator

- examines personal and professional values
- demonstrates a personal and professional code of ethics
- demonstrates values, beliefs, and attitudes that inspire others to higher levels of performance
- serves as a role model
- accepts responsibility for school operations
- considers the impact of one's administrative practices on others
- uses the influence of the office to enhance the educational program rather than for personal gain
- treats people fairly, equitably, and with dignity and respect
- protects the rights and confidentiality of students and staff
- demonstrates appreciation for, and sensitivity to, the diversity in the school community
- recognizes and respects the legitimate authority of others
- examines and considers the prevailing values of the diverse school community
- expects that others in the school community will demonstrate integrity and exercise ethical behavior
- opens the school to public scrutiny
- fulfills legal and contractual obligations
- applies laws and procedures fairly, wisely, and considerately

Standard 6

A school administrator is an educational leader who promotes the success of all students by understanding, responding to, and influencing the larger political, social, economic, legal, and cultural context.

Knowledge. The administrator has knowledge and understanding of

- principles of representative governance that undergird the system of American schools
- the role of public education in developing and renewing a democratic society and an economically productive nation
- the law as related to education and schooling
- the political, social, cultural, and economic systems and processes that have an impact on schools

- models and strategies of change and conflict resolution as applied to the larger political, social, cultural, and economic contexts of schooling
- global issues and forces affecting teaching and learning
- the dynamics of policy development and advocacy under our democratic political system
- the importance of diversity and equity in a democratic society

Dispositions. The administrator believes in, values, and is committed to

- education as a key to opportunity and social mobility
- recognizing a variety of ideas, values, and cultures
- importance of a continuing dialogue with other decision makers affecting education
- actively participating in the political and policy-making context in the service of education
- using legal systems to protect student rights and to improve student opportunities

Performances. The administrator facilitates processes and engages in activities ensuring that

- the environment in which schools operate is influenced on behalf of students and their families
- communication occurs among the school community concerning trends, issues, and potential changes in the environment in which schools operate
- there is ongoing dialogue with representatives of diverse community groups
- the school community works within the framework of policies, laws, and regulations enacted by local, state, and federal authorities
- public policy is shaped to provide quality education for students
- lines of communication are developed with decision makers outside the school community

Council of Chief State School Officers, One Massachusetts Avenue, NW, Suite 700, Washington, DC 20001-1431, voice: 202.408.5505 · fax: 202.408.8072.

National Council for Accreditation of Teacher Education (NCATE): Advanced Programs in Educational Leadership for Principals, Superintendents, Curriculum Directors, and Supervisors

These standards were developed by the National Policy Board for Educational Administration (NPBEA) on behalf of the agency that accredits schools and colleges of education, The National Council for Accreditation of Teacher Education (NCATE), to judge the quality of graduate programs that prepare school administrators. NCATE requires that guidelines be revised and resubmitted every five years. Between publication of the Educational Leadership Constituent Council's *Guidelines for Advanced Programs in Educational Leadership* in 1995 and the revision, NCATE delineated a new direction for accreditation. This new direction, to be implemented in Spring 2003, calls for a more results-focused orientation. Because the Interstate School Leaders Licensure Consortium (ISLCC) standards and the ELCC guidelines were similar, the two sets of criteria were combined in these new standards. These new standards provide assessment for school building leadership and for school district leadership. The criteria used for this book are Standards for School District Leadership. Complete standards can be found at www.ncate.org.

STANDARD 1

Candidates who complete the program are educational leaders who have the knowledge and ability to promote the success of all students

---

*Reprinted from Professional Standards for the Accreditation of Schools, Colleges, and Departments of Education (7/25/02) with permission of the National Council for Accreditation of Teacher Education, Washington, D.C. All rights reserved.

by facilitating the development, articulation, implementation, and stewardship of a school or district vision of learning supported by the school community.

Develop a Vision

- Develop and demonstrate the skills needed to work with a board of education to facilitate the development of a vision of learning for a school district that promotes the success of all students.
- Base development of the vision on relevant knowledge and theories applicable to school-level leaders applied to a school district context.
- Use data-based research strategies to create a vision that takes into account the diversity of learners in a district.
- Demonstrate knowledge of ways to use a district's vision to mobilize additional resources to support the vision.

Articulate a Vision

- Demonstrate the ability to articulate the components of this vision for a district and the leadership processes necessary to implement and support the vision.
- Demonstrate the ability to use data-based research strategies and strategic planning processes that focus on student learning to develop a vision, drawing on relevant information sources such as student assessment results, student and family demographic data, and an analysis of community needs.
- Demonstrate the ability to communicate the vision to school boards, staff, parents, students, and community members through the use of symbols, ceremonies, stories, and other activities.

Implement a Vision

- Demonstrate the ability to plan programs to motivate staff, students, and families to achieve a school district's vision.
- Design research-based processes to effectively implement a district vision throughout an entire school district and community.

Steward a Vision

- Demonstrate the ability to align and, as necessary, redesign administrative policies and practices required for full implementation of a district vision.
- Understand the theory and research related to organizational and educational leadership and engage in the collection, organization, and analysis of a variety of information, including student performance data, required to assess progress toward a district's vision, mission, and goals.

Promote Community Involvement in the Vision

- Demonstrate the ability to bring together and communicate effectively with stakeholders within the district and the larger community concerning implementation and realization of the vision.

STANDARD 2

Candidates who complete the program are educational leaders who have the knowledge and ability to promote the success of all students by promoting a positive school culture, providing an effective instructional program, applying best practice to student learning, and designing comprehensive professional growth plans for staff.

Promote Positive School Culture

- Develop a sustained approach to improve and maintain a positive district culture for learning that capitalizes on multiple aspects of diversity to meet the learning needs of all students.

Provide Effective Instructional Program

- Demonstrate an understanding of a variety of instructional research methodologies and analyze the comparable strengths and weaknesses of each method.

- An ability to use qualitative and quantitative data, appropriate research methods, technology, and information systems to develop a long-range plan for a district that assesses the district's improvement and accountability systems.
- Demonstrate the ability to use and promote technology and information systems to enrich district curriculum and instruction, monitor instructional practices, and provide assistance to administrators who have needs for improvement.
- Demonstrate the ability to allocate and justify resources to sustain the instructional program.

Apply Best Practice to Student Learning

- Demonstrate the ability to facilitate and to engage in activities that use best practices and sound educational research to improve instructional programs.
- Demonstrate an ability to assist school and district personnel in understanding and applying best practices for student learning.
- Understand and can apply human development theory, proven learning, and motivational theories, and concern for diversity to the learning process.
- Understand how to use appropriate research strategies to profile student performance in a district and to analyze differences among subgroups.

Design Comprehensive Professional Growth Plans

- Demonstrate knowledge of adult learning strategies and the ability to apply technology and research to professional development design focusing on authentic problems and tasks, mentoring, coaching, conferencing, and other techniques that promote new knowledge and skills in the workplace.
- Demonstrate the ability to use strategies such as observations and collaborative reflection to help form comprehensive professional growth plans with district and school personnel.
- Develop personal professional growth plans that reflect commitment to lifelong learning and best practices.

STANDARD 3

Candidates who complete the program are educational leaders who have the knowledge and ability to promote the success of all students by managing the organization, operations, and resources in a way that promotes a safe, efficient, and effective learning environment.

Manage the Organization

- Demonstrate the ability to use research-based knowledge of learning, teaching, student development, organizational development, and data management to optimize learning for all students.
- Demonstrate effective organization of fiscal, human, and material resources, giving priority to student learning and safety, and demonstrating an understanding of district budgeting processes and fiduciary responsibilities.
- Demonstrate the ability to manage time effectively and to deploy financial and human resources in a way that promotes student achievement.
- Demonstrate the ability to organize a district based on indicators of equity, effectiveness, and efficiency and can apply legal principles that promote educational equity.
- Demonstrate an understanding of how to apply legal principles to promote educational equity and provide safe, effective, and efficient facilities.

Manage Operations

- Demonstrate the ability to involve stakeholders in aligning resources and priorities to maximize ownership and accountability.
- Use appropriate and effective needs assessment, research-based data, and group process skills to build consensus, communicate, and resolve conflicts in order to align resources with the district vision.
- Develop staff communication plans for integrating district's schools and divisions.
- Develop a plan to promote and to support community collaboration among district personnel.

Manage Resources

- Use problem-solving skills and knowledge of strategic, long-range, and operational planning (including applications of technology) in the effective, legal, and equitable use of fiscal, human, and material resource allocation that focuses on teaching and learning.
- Creatively seek new resources to facilitate learning.
- Apply an understanding of school district finance structures and models to ensure that adequate financial resources are allocated equitably for the district.
- Apply and assess current technologies for management, business procedures, and scheduling.

STANDARD 4

Candidates who complete the program are educational leaders who have the knowledge and ability to promote the success of all students by collaborating with families and other community members, responding to diverse community interests and needs, and mobilizing community resources.

Collaborate with Families and Other Community Members

- Demonstrate the ability to facilitate the planning and implementation of programs and services that bring together the resources of families and the community to positively affect student learning.
- Demonstrate an ability to use public information and research-based knowledge of issues and trends to collaborate with community members and community organizations to have a positive effect on student learning.
- Apply an understanding of community relations models, marketing strategies and processes, data-driven decision making, and communication theory to craft frameworks for school, business, community, government, and higher education partnerships.
- Demonstrate an ability to develop and implement a plan for nurturing relationships with community leaders and reaching out to different business, religious, political, and service organizations to strengthen programs and support district goals.

- Demonstrate the ability to involve community members, groups, and other stakeholders in district decision making, reflecting an understanding of strategies to capitalize on the district's integral role in the larger community.
- Demonstrate the ability to collaborate with community agencies to integrate health, social, and other services in the schools to address student and family conditions that affect learning.
- Demonstrate the ability to conduct community relations that reflect knowledge of effective media relations and that models effective media relations practices.
- Develop and implement strategies that support the involvement of families in the education of their children that reinforces for district staff a belief that families have the best interests of their children in mind.

Respond to Community Interests and Needs

- Facilitate and engage in activities that reflect an ability to inform district decision making by collecting and organizing formal and informal information from multiple stakeholders.
- Demonstrate the ability to promote maximum involvement with and visibility within the community.
- Demonstrate the ability to interact effectively with individuals and groups that reflect conflicting perspectives.
- Demonstrate the ability to effectively and appropriately assess, research, and plan for diverse district and community conditions and dynamics and capitalize on the diversity of the community to improve district performance and student achievement.
- Demonstrate the ability to advocate for students with special and exceptional needs.

Mobilize Community Resources

- Demonstrate an understanding of and ability to use community resources, including youth services that enhance student achievement, to solve district problems, and accomplish district goals.
- Demonstrate how to use district resources for the community to solve issues of joint concern.

- Demonstrate an understanding of ways to use public resources and funds appropriately and effectively to encourage communities to provide new resources to address emerging student problems.

STANDARD 5

Candidates who complete the program are educational leaders who have the knowledge and ability to promote the success of all students by acting with integrity, with fairness, and in an ethical manner.

Act with Integrity

- Demonstrate a respect for the rights of others with regard to confidentiality and dignity and engage in honest interactions.

Act Fairly

- Demonstrate the ability to combine impartiality, sensitivity to student diversity, and ethical considerations in their interactions with others.

Act Ethically

- Make and explain decisions based on ethical and legal principles.

STANDARD 6

Candidates who complete the program are educational leaders who have the knowledge and ability to promote the success of all students by understanding, responding to, and influencing the larger political, social, economic, legal, and cultural context.

Understand the Larger Context

- Demonstrate the ability to use appropriate research methods, theories, and concepts to improve district operations.

- Demonstrate an understanding of the complex causes of poverty and other disadvantages and their effects on families, communities, children, and learning.
- Demonstrate an understanding of the policies, laws, and regulations enacted by local, state, and federal authorities affecting a specific district.
- Explain the system for financing public schools and its effects on the equitable distribution of educational opportunities within a district.
- Demonstrate the ability to work with political leaders at the local, state, and national level.
- Apply an understanding of how specific laws at the local, state, and federal level affect school districts and residents.
- Espouse positions in response to proposed policy changes that would benefit or harm districts, and explain how proposed policies and laws might improve educational and social opportunities for specific communities.

Respond to the Larger Context

- Demonstrate the ability to engage students, parents, members of the school board, and other community members in advocating for adoption of improved policies and laws.
- Apply understanding of the larger political, social, economic, legal, and cultural context to develop activities and policies that benefit their district and its students.
- Demonstrate the ability to communicate regularly with all segments of the district community concerning trends, issues, and policies affecting the district.

Influence the Larger Context

- Demonstrate an understanding of how to develop lines of communication with local, state, and federal authorities, and actively advocate for improved policies, laws, and regulations affecting a specific district, both directly and through organizations representing schools, educators, or others with similar interests.

- Demonstrate the ability to advocate for policies and programs that promote equitable learning opportunities and success for all students, regardless of socioeconomic background, ethnicity, gender, disability, or other individual characteristics.

Prepared by National Policy Board for Educational Administration (NPBEA) for the Educational Leadership Constituent Council (ELCC)

Index

About the Authors

Sandra Lowery is a former public school superintendent. She is currently a full professor and chair of the Department of Secondary Education and Educational Leadership at Stephen F. Austin State University in Nacogdoches, Texas.

Sandra Harris is an educator with experience in K–12 public and private. She is currently assistant professor in the Department of Secondary Education and Educational Leadership at Stephen F. Austin State University in Nacogdoches, Texas.